California Politics & Government

California Politics & Government

A Practical Approach

FOURTEENTH EDITION

LARRY N. GERSTON
San Jose State University

TERRY CHRISTENSEN
San Jose State University

 CENGAGE

Australia • Brazil • Mexico • Singapore • United Kingdom • United States

CENGAGE

California Politics & Government: A Practical Approach, **Fourteenth Edition**

Larry N. Gerston and Terry Christensen

Executive Director of Development: Carolyn Lewis

Product Manager: Bradley Potthoff

Production Manager: Lauren Maclachlan

Vendor Content Project Manager: Andrea Stefanowicz, Lumina Datamatics, Inc.

Senior Content Project Manager: Andrea Wagner

Art Director: Heather Marshall, Lumina Datamatics, Inc.

IP Project Manager: Betsy Hathaway

Art and Cover Direction, Production Management, and Composition: Lumina Datamatics, Inc.

Manufacturing Planner: Fola Orekoya

Cover Image: Rada Photos/ Shutterstock.com, iStockphoto. com/Elizabeth Parodi, iStockphoto.com/slobo

For product information and technology assistance, contact us at **Cengage Customer & Sales Support, 1-800-354-9706 or support.cengage.com.**

For permission to use material from this text or product, submit all requests online at **www.cengage.com/permissions.**

Library of Congress Control Number: 2016956954

ISBN-13: 978-1-305-95349-9

Cengage
20 Channel Street
Boston, MA 02210
USA

Cengage is a leading provider of customized learning solutions with employees residing in nearly 40 different countries and sales in more than 125 countries around the world. Find your local representative at: **www.cengage.com.**

Cengage products are represented in Canada by Nelson Education, Ltd.

To learn more about Cengage platforms and services, register or access your online learning solution, or purchase materials for your course, visit **www.cengage.com.**

*To the future of Gia Gabriella Gerston and the memories
of Anna and Teter Christensen and Tillie and Chester Welliever*

Contents

8   Taxing and Spending: Budgetary Politics and Policies   111

Preface

Imagine yourself strapped in on a rollercoaster that soars, dips, and turns at incredible speeds and gravitational force, leaving you breathless as it comes to a stop. That physical experience is not so far from the gyrations of California politics, except that our political rollercoaster never stops. The fast-changing political setting in California is almost mind boggling in depth and direction. Here, an endless cast of participants struggle to solve complex issues in an environment teeming with forces pushing and pulling for resolution.

People often ask us why we write *California Politics & Government* every two years. That's a fair question, given that few texts are typically written with such a short publication schedule. But California is hardly a typical place, where politics meander along a predictably slow-moving political river. Here, politics splash the state with fits and starts, clashes and confusion, urgency and resistance.

But there is so much more. Along with our bedrock institutions, California has a kaleidoscopic combination of policy issues that constantly compete for attention. Some issues, such as educational finance, seem to be resolved one moment, only to appear again at another. Other issues, such as the state's massive prison realignment program and recent sentence restructuring laws, seem to point the state in a new direction. Predictably, the state's most troublesome problems such as water, land use, taxation, and environmental protection, to name a few, stagger from one year to the next, with little agreement among the major stakeholders, which leaves the state in knots.

In addition to the panoply of resolved and unresolved issues, California's political colors continue to change. Today, California is less white and more blue. By that, we mean non-whites now form a solid majority of the state's residents and have benefited from increasing numbers of election victories. At the same time, Democrats have grown disproportionately compared to Republicans, making California virtually a one-party state. As we see it, the first trend is not likely to change; diversity will march on as a compelling state characteristic. But political party dominance is bit more fickle; only time will tell whether Democrats continue as the prevailing political party in the Golden State.

All of these factors and more provide the rationale for why we write this book every two years. Much like a public official running for reelection the day after he or she wins office, the day after we complete one edition, we are working on the next. It's the only way we know how to produce an up-to-date volume about an ever-changing state. In this way, the fourteenth edition of *California Politics & Government* is no different than its predecessors. As in the past, we cover the nuts and bolts of our state's political machinery, taking care to update the roles of our institutions at the state and local levels as well as their interaction with the federal government. Equally important, we focus on the current occupants of the state's offices, bearing in mind term limits for most. After all, it's hard to understand a state government if we don't know something about the officeholders, as well as the major players seeking to influence their decisions.

Virtually every election changes the state's leadership elements, which is yet another reason why we strive to be current, and why this book contains the results of the 2016 general election. If the past is any guide to the future, the most recent election outcomes, including Donald Trump's ascension to the presidency, will form the framework of what happens—or fails to happen—over the next two years.

Our goal is to better acquaint you with this place we know as California, for without understanding how the state works, there is little we can do about it. We have not embarked on this journey alone. Our colleagues in politics, the media, and elected office, as well as fellow academics, have offered valuable counsel, knowledge, and insights. We especially thank the following reviewers, whose comments have helped us prepare this edition: Paul E. Frank, Ph.D, Sacramento City College, and Maria Sampanis, California State University, Sacramento. Most of all, we continue to learn from our students, whose penetrating questions and observations inspire us to explore issues we might not have considered otherwise. Over the years, many have gone on to political careers in local, state, and federal offices, leaving us with the strong belief that California's best days are ahead.

Finally, we are indebted to the attentive team at Cengage, who artfully managed an incredibly tight production schedule that allowed the publication of the book within weeks of the November 8, 2016, election. They include Bradley Potthoff, Product Manager; Andrea Stefanowicz, Vendor Content Project Manager; and Andrea Wagner, Senior Content Project Manager. All of these people were instrumental in completing the project. Of course, we alone assume responsibility for the contents of the final product.

Larry N. Gerston and Terry Christensen

About the Authors

Larry N. Gerston, professor emeritus of political science at San Jose State University, interacts with the political process as both an author and an observer. As an author, he has written eleven academic books in addition to *California Politics and Government: A Practical Approach,* including *Making Public Policy: From Conflict to Resolution* (1983), *Politics in the Golden State* (with Terry Christensen, 1984), *The Deregulated Society* (with Cynthia Fraleigh and Robert Schwab, 1988), *American Government: Politics, Process and Policies* (1993), *Public Policy: Process and Principles (1987), Public Policymaking in a Democratic Society: A Guide to Civic Engagement* (2002), *Recall! California's Political Earthquake (with Terry Christensen, 2004), American Federalism: A Concise Introduction* (2007), *Confronting Reality: Ten Issues Threatening to Implode American Society and How We Can Fix It* (2009), *Not So Golden After All: The Rise and Fall of California* (2012), and *Reviving Citizen Engagement: Policies to Renew National Community* (2015). Gerston serves as the political analyst for NBC11, a San Francisco Bay Area television station, where he appears on a regular basis. He has written more than 125 op-ed pieces for newspapers throughout the nation and speaks often on issues such as civic engagement and political empowerment.

Terry Christensen is a San Jose State University professor emeritus of political science. Among his other awards for scholarship and service to the university, he was named Outstanding Professor in 1998. He is the author or co-author of nine books and frequent newspaper op-ed pieces. Local and national media regularly call on him for analysis of politics in California and Silicon Valley. In addition to other books co-authored with Larry Gerston, his works include *Projecting Politics: Political Messages in American Films* (2005), co-authored by Peter Haas, and *Local Politics: A Practical Guide to Governing at the Grassroots* (2006), co-authored by Tom Hogen-Esch. Christensen is experienced in practical politics at the local level as an advocate of policy proposals, an adviser to grassroots groups, and an adviser and mentor to candidates for local office—many of whom are his former students. He has served on numerous civic committees and commissions. He was the founding executive director of CommUniverCity San Jose (www.cucsj.org), a partnership between the City of San Jose, San Jose State University, and adjacent neighborhoods. Through CommUniverCity, hundreds of students are learning about life and politics in their community through service projects selected by neighborhood residents and supported by the city.

SUPPLEMENTS FOR INSTRUCTORS

Instructor's Manual with Test Bank Online for Gerston/Christensen
California Politics and Government: A Practical Approach, **14e**

- ISBN: 9781305953512

This password-protected Instructor's Manual and Test Bank are accessible by logging into your account at www.cengage.com/login

1

California's People, Economy, and Politics: Yesterday, Today, and Tomorrow

LEARNING OBJECTIVES

1.1 Describe changes in California's population in the eighteenth and nineteenth centuries.

1.2 Discuss the rise and fall of California's political machine.

1.3 Explain how Progressive reforms shape California politics today.

1.4 Summarize demographic change in the twentieth century and its impact today.

1.5 Analyze the impacts of economic diversity and regional differences on California politics.

How can we understand the way a political system functions in a place like California? With a population of 39 million, California is larger than many independent nations. With an economy generating a gross domestic product (GDP) of $2.5 trillion in 2015, California would rank sixth in the world if it were a separate nation. And California is not just big; it's also the most ethnically diverse state in the United States (and one of the most ethnically diverse places in the world), and its economy is also highly diversified.

And that's just the beginning. The economy booms, then goes bust. Political leaders rise and fall precipitously. Wealthy candidates and special interests are accused of "buying" elections. State government stalls in gridlock, resulting in issues being referred to the voters, who are often asked to make decisions about complex and sometimes obscure issues. Our problems seem overwhelming—a failing education system, aging infrastructure (such as roads and water storage facilities), a shortage of affordable housing, crushing poverty, budget deficits, and political leadership that sometimes doesn't seem focused on solving these problem and others.[1]

But, however confusing California politics may seem, it is serious business that affects us all, and it can be understood by examining the history and present characteristics of our state. The basic structures of California government as it operates today, including the executive, legislature, and judiciary, were established in the state constitutions of 1849 and 1879. At the beginning of the twentieth century, the Progressive movement constrained California's political parties and created direct democracy, the system that enables voters to make decisions about specific issues and policies. This history helps explain our present. But another part of that history is our constantly changing population and economy. Wave after wave of immigrants have made California a diverse, multicultural society, while new technologies repeatedly transform the state's economy. The resulting disparate demographic and economic interests compete for the benefits and protections conferred by government and thus shape the state's politics. We can understand California today—and tomorrow—by learning about its past and about the development of the competing interests within the state.

FROM THE FIRST CALIFORNIANS TO STATEHOOD[2]

The first Californians were probably immigrants like the rest of us. Archaeologists believe that the ancestors of American Indians crossed an ice or land bridge or traveled by sea from Asia to Alaska thousands of years ago, and then headed south. Europeans began exploring the California coast in the early 1500s, but colonization didn't start until 1769, when the Spanish established a string of missions and military outposts. The Native American population then numbered about 300,000, most living near the coast.

Many native Californians were brought to the missions as Catholic converts and workers, but violence, European diseases, and the destruction of the native culture reduced their numbers to about 100,000 by 1849. Entire tribes were wiped out, and the Indian population continued to diminish throughout the nineteenth century. Today, less than 1 percent of California's population is Native American, many of whom feel alienated from a society that has overwhelmed their peoples, cultures, and traditions. Poverty, a chronic condition in the past, has been alleviated somewhat by the development of casinos on native lands, a phenomenon that has also made some tribes major players in state politics.

Apart from building missions, the Spaniards did little to develop their faraway possession. Not much changed when Mexico (which by now included California) declared independence from Spain in 1822. A few thousand Mexicans quietly raised cattle on vast ranches and built small towns around central plazas.

Meanwhile, advocates of expansion in the United States coveted California's rich lands and access to the Pacific Ocean. When Mexico and the United States went to war over Texas in 1846, Yankee immigrants in California seized the moment and declared independence from Mexico. The United States won the war, and Mexico surrendered its claim to lands extending from Texas to California. By this time, foreigners already outnumbered Californians of Spanish or Mexican ancestry 9,000 to 7,500.

Gold was discovered in 1848, and the '49ers who started arriving in hordes the next year brought the nonnative population to 264,000 by 1852. Many immigrants came directly from Europe. The first Chinese people also arrived to work in the mines, which yielded more than a billion dollars' worth of gold in five years.

The new Californians soon took political action. A constitutional convention consisting of forty-eight delegates (only seven of whom were native Californians) assembled the **Constitution of 1849** by cutting and pasting from the constitutions of existing states; the convention requested statehood, which the U.S. Congress quickly granted. The constitutional structure of the new state approximated what we have today, with a two-house legislature; a supreme court; and an executive branch consisting of a governor, lieutenant governor, controller, attorney general, and superintendent of public instruction. The constitution also included a bill of rights, but only white males were allowed to vote. California's Chinese, African American, and Native American residents were soon prohibited by law from owning land, testifying in court, or attending public schools.

The voters approved the constitution, and San Jose became the first state capital. With housing in short supply, many newly elected legislators had to lodge in tents, and the primitive living conditions were exacerbated by heavy rain and flooding. The state capital soon moved on to Vallejo and Benicia, finally settling in 1854 in Sacramento—closer to the gold fields.

As the Gold Rush ended, a land rush began. Small homesteads were common in other states because of federal ownership and allocation of land, but California had been divided into huge tracts by Spanish and Mexican land grants. As early as 1870, a few hundred men owned most of the farmland. Their ranches were the forerunners of the agribusiness corporations of today, and as the mainstay of the state's economy, they exercised even more clout than their modern successors.

In less than fifty years, California had belonged to three different nations. During the same period, its economy and population had changed dramatically as hundreds of thousands of immigrants from all over the world came to claim their share of the "Golden State." The pattern of a rapidly evolving, multicultural polity was set.

RAILROADS, MACHINES, AND REFORM

Technology wrought the next transformation in the form of railroads. In 1861, Sacramento merchants led by Leland Stanford founded the company that would become the **Southern Pacific Railroad**. They persuaded Congress to provide millions of dollars in land grants and loan subsidies for a railroad linking

California with the eastern United States, thus greatly expanding the market for California's products. Stanford became governor and used his influence to provide state assistance. Cities and counties also contributed—under the threat of being bypassed by the railroad. To obtain workers at cheap rates, the railroad builders imported 15,000 Chinese laborers.

When the transcontinental track was completed in 1869, the Southern Pacific expanded its system throughout the state by building new lines and buying up existing ones. The railroad crushed competitors by cutting shipping charges, and by the 1880s it had become the state's dominant transportation company, as well as its largest private landowner, with 11 percent of the entire state. With its business agents doubling as political representatives in almost every California city and county, the Southern Pacific soon developed a formidable political machine. "The Octopus," as novelist Frank Norris called the railroad,[3] placed allies in state and local offices through its control of both the Republican and Democratic parties. Once there, these officials protected the interests of the Southern Pacific if they wanted to continue in office. County tax assessors who were supported by the political machine set favorable tax rates for the railroad and its allies, while the machine-controlled legislature ensured a hands-off policy by state government.

People in small towns and rural areas who were unwilling to support the machine lost jobs, businesses, and other benefits. Some moved to cities, especially San Francisco, where manufacturing jobs were available. Chinese workers who had been brought to California to build the railroad also sought work in the cities when the railroad was completed. But when a depression in the 1870s made jobs scarce, the Chinese faced hostile treatment from those who came earlier. Irish immigrants, blaming economic difficulties on the Chinese and the railroad machine, became the core of a new political organization they christened the **Workingmen's Party**.

Meanwhile, small farmers who felt oppressed by the railroad united through the Grange movement. In 1879, the Grangers and the Workingmen's Party called California's second constitutional convention in hopes of breaking the railroad's hold on the state. The **Constitution of 1879** mandated regulation of railroads, utilities, banks, and corporations. An elected State Board of Equalization was set up to ensure the fairness of local tax assessments on railroads and their friends, as well as their enemies. The new constitution also prohibited the Chinese from owning land, voting, or working for state or local government.

The railroad soon reclaimed power, however, by taking control of the agencies that were created to regulate it. Nonetheless, efforts to regulate big business and control racial relations became recurring themes in California life and politics, and much of the Constitution of 1879 remains intact today.

The growth fostered by the railroad eventually produced a new middle class of merchants, doctors, lawyers, teachers, and skilled workers who were not dependent on the railroad. They objected to the corrupt practices and favoritism of the railroad's machine, which they claimed was restraining economic development in their communities. This new middle class demanded honesty and competence, which they called "good government." In 1907, some of these crusaders established the Lincoln-Roosevelt League, a reform group within the Republican Party, and became part of the national Progressive movement. Their leader,

Hiram Johnson, was elected governor in 1910; they also captured control of the state legislature.

To break the power of the machine, the **Progressives** introduced a wave of reforms that shape California politics to this day. Predictably, they created a new regulatory agency for the railroads and utilities, the Public Utilities Commission (PUC). Most of their reforms, however, were aimed at weakening the political parties as tools of bosses and machines. Instead of party bosses handpicking candidates at party conventions, the voters now were given the power to select their party's nominees for office in primary elections. Cross-filing further diluted party power by allowing candidates to file for and win the nominations of more than one political party. City and county elections were made "nonpartisan" by removing party labels from local ballots altogether. The Progressives also created a civil service system to select state employees on the basis of their qualifications rather than their political connections.

Finally, the Progressives introduced direct democracy, which allowed the voters to amend the constitution, create laws through initiatives, repeal laws through referenda, and recall (remove) elected officials before their terms expired. Supporters of an initiative, referendum, or recall must circulate petitions and collect a specified number of signatures of registered voters before it goes to the voters.

Like the Workingmen's Party before them, the Progressives were concerned about immigration. Antagonism toward recent Japanese immigrants (who numbered 72,000 by 1910) resulted in Progressive support for a ban on land ownership by "aliens" and the National Immigration Act of 1924, which halted Asian immigration. Other, more positive changes by the Progressives included giving women the right to vote, passing child labor and workers' compensation laws, and implementing conservation programs to protect natural resources.

As a result of these reforms, the railroad's political machine eventually died, although California's increasingly diverse economy also weakened the machine, as the emerging oil, automobile, and trucking industries gave the state alternative means of transportation and shipping. These and other growing industries ultimately restructured economic and political power in California.

The reform movement waned in the 1920s, but the Progressive legacy of weak political parties and direct democracy opened up California's politics to its citizens, as well as to powerful interest groups and individual candidates with strong personalities. A long and detailed constitution is also part of the legacy. The Progressives instituted their reforms by amending (and thus lengthening) the Constitution of 1879 rather than calling for a new constitutional convention. Direct democracy subsequently enabled voters and interest groups to amend the constitution, constantly adding to its length.

THE DEPRESSION AND WORLD WAR II

California's population grew by more than 2 million in the 1920s (see Table 1.1). Many newcomers headed for Los Angeles, where employment

TABLE 1.1 California's Population Growth

Year	Population	Percentage of U.S. Population
1850	93,000	0.4
1900	1,485,000	2.0
1950	10,643,000	7.0
1970	20,039,000	9.8
1990	29,733,000	11.7
2010	37,253,956	12.0
2016	39,309,017	12.2

SOURCE: U.S. Census.

opportunities in shipping, filmmaking, and manufacturing (of clothing, automobiles, and aircraft) abounded. Then came the Great Depression of the 1930s, which saw the unemployment rate soar from 3 percent in 1925 to 33 percent by 1933. Even so, more than a million people came to California in the 1930s, including thousands of poor white immigrants from the "dust bowl" of the drought-impacted Midwest. Immortalized by John Steinbeck's *The Grapes of Wrath*, rather than welcoming them, the state set up roadblocks and tried to ban indigent migrants. Many wandered through California's great Central Valley in search of work, displacing Mexicans—who earlier had supplanted the Chinese and Japanese—as farm workers. Racial antagonism ran high, and many Mexicans were arbitrarily sent back to Mexico. Labor unrest reached a crescendo in the early 1930s, as workers on farms, in canneries, and on the docks of San Francisco and Los Angeles fought for higher wages and an eight-hour workday.

The immigrants and union activists of this era changed California politics by voting for Democrats, thus challenging Republican dominance of the state. Thanks to the Depression and President Franklin Roosevelt's popular New Deal, Democrats become California's majority party in registration. Winning elections proved more difficult, however. The Democrats won the governorship in 1938, but their candidate, Culbert Olson, was the only Democratic winner between 1894 and 1958.

During the Depression, the state and federal governments invested heavily in California's future, building the Golden Gate Bridge (in just four years!) and the Central Valley Project, whose dams and canals brought water to the desert and reaffirmed agriculture as a mainstay of California's economy. Then, during World War II, the federal government spent $35 billion in California, creating 500,000 defense industry jobs. California's radio, electronics, and aircraft industries grew at phenomenal rates. The jobs brought new immigrants, including many African Americans, whose proportion of the state's population quadrupled during the 1940s.

Meanwhile, California's Japanese and Mexican American residents became victims of racial conflict. During the war, 120,000 Japanese Americans, suspected of loyalty to their ancestral homeland, were sent to prison camps (officially called "internment centers"). Antagonism toward Mexican Americans resulted in the Zoot Suit Riots in Los Angeles in 1943, when white sailors and police attacked Mexican Americans who were wearing the suits they favored, featuring long jackets with wide lapels, padded shoulders, and high-waisted, pegged pants.

Although the voters chose a Democratic governor during the Great Depression, they returned to the Republican fold as the economy revived. **Earl Warren**, one of a new breed of moderate Republicans, was elected governor in 1942, 1946, and 1950. Warren used cross-filing to win the nominations of both parties and staked out a relationship with the voters that he claimed was above party politics. A classic example of California's personality-oriented politics, Warren left the state in 1953 to become chief justice of the U.S. Supreme Court.

GROWTH, CHANGE, AND POLITICAL TURMOIL

After Warren, the Republican Party fell into disarray due to infighting. Californians elected a Democratic governor, **Edmund G. "Pat" Brown**, and a Democratic majority in the state legislature in 1958. To prevent Republicans like Warren from taking advantage of cross-filing again, the state's new leaders quickly repealed that electoral device.

In control of both the governor's office and the legislature for the first time in the twentieth century, Democrats moved aggressively to develop the state's infrastructure. Completion of the massive California Water Project, construction of the state highway network, and creation of an unparalleled higher education system helped accommodate the growing population and stimulated the economy. Meanwhile, in the 1960s, black and Latino minorities became more assertive, pushing for civil rights, desegregation of schools, access to higher education, and improved treatment for California's predominantly Latino farm workers.

The demands of minority groups alienated some white voters, however, and the Democratic programs were expensive. After opening their purse strings during the eight-year tenure of Pat Brown, Californians became more cautious about the state's direction. Race riots precipitated by police brutality in Los Angeles, along with student unrest over the Vietnam War, also turned the voters against liberal Democrats such as Brown.

In 1966, Republican **Ronald Reagan** was elected governor; he moved the state in a more conservative direction before going on to serve as president. His successor as governor, Democrat **Edmund G. "Jerry" Brown, Jr.**, was the son of the earlier governor Brown and a liberal on social issues. Like Reagan, however, the younger Brown led California away from spending on growth-inducing infrastructure, such as highways and schools. In 1978, the voters solidified this change with the watershed tax-cutting initiative, Proposition 13 (see Chapter 8). Although Democrats still outnumbered Republicans among registered voters, California elected Republican governors from 1982 to 1998 (see Chapter 7).

Democrat **Gray Davis** was elected in 1998 and reelected in 2002 despite voter concerns about an energy crisis, a recession, and a growing budget deficit. As a consequence of these crises and what some perceived as an arrogant attitude, Davis faced an unprecedented recall election in October 2003. The voters removed him from office and replaced him with Republican **Arnold Schwarzenegger**. Then, in 2010, former governor Jerry Brown was elected yet again in a dramatic comeback, making history as being both the youngest and the oldest governor of California.

While Schwarzenegger and other Republicans have managed to win gubernatorial elections, Californians have voted for Democrats in every presidential election since 1988, and Democrats have also had consistent success in the state legislature and the congressional delegation, where they have dominated since 1960. In addition to their legislative majorities, Democrats have controlled every statewide office since 2010.

Meanwhile, the voters have become increasingly involved in policy making by initiatives and referenda (see Chapter 2) as well as **constitutional amendments**, which can be placed on the ballot by a two-thirds vote of the state legislature or by citizen petition and which require voter approval. California's Constitution of 1879 has been amended over 500 times (the U.S. Constitution includes just twenty-seven amendments).

All through these years, the state's population continued to grow, outpacing most other states so much that the California delegation to the U.S. House of Representatives now numbers fifty-three—more than twenty-one other states combined. Much of this growth was the result of a new wave of immigrants facilitated by more flexible national laws during the 1960s and 1970s. Immigration from Asia—especially from Southeast Asia after the Vietnam War—increased greatly. A national amnesty for undocumented residents signed by President Ronald Reagan in 1986 also enabled many Mexicans to gain citizenship and bring their families from Mexico. In all, 85 percent of the 6 million newcomers and births in California in the 1980s were Asian, Latino, or black. Growth slowed in the 1990s, as 2 million more people left the state than came to it from other states, but California's population continued to increase as a result of births and immigration from abroad. In 1990, whites made up 57 percent of the state's population; by 2014, they were 39 percent.

Constantly increasing diversity enlivened California's culture and provided a steady flow of new workers, but it also increased tensions. Some affluent Californians retreated to gated communities; others fled the state. Racial conflict broke out between gangs on the streets and in prisons. As in difficult economic times throughout California history, many Californians blamed immigrants, especially those who were here illegally, for their problems during the recession of the early 1990s. A series of ballot measures raised divisive race-related issues such as illegal immigration, bilingualism, and affirmative action. The issue of immigration inflames California politics to this day, although the increasing electoral clout of minorities has provided some balance.

CALIFORNIA TODAY

As noted at the beginning of this chapter, if California were an independent nation, its economy would rank sixth in the world, with an annual GDP of over $2.4 trillion. Much of the state's strength stems from its economic diversity (see Table 1.2). The elements of this diversity also constitute powerful political interests in state politics.

Half of California—mostly desert and mountains—is owned by the state and federal governments. Outside the cities, a few big corporations control much of the state's rich farmlands. These enormous agribusinesses make California the nation's leading farm state, with over 80,000 farms producing more than 400 commodities, including nearly half of the vegetables, fruits, and nuts and 21 percent of the dairy products consumed nationally. Grapes and wine are also top products, with thousands of growers and 4,285 wineries.

State politics affects this huge economic force in many ways, but most notably in labor relations, environmental regulation, and water supply. Farmers and their employees have battled for decades over issues ranging from wages to safety. Beginning in the 1960s, under the leadership of Cesar Chavez and the United Farm Workers union, laborers organized. Supported by public boycotts

T A B L E 1.2 California's Economy

Industrial Sector	Employees	Amount (in millions of $)
Professional and business services	2,549,500	327,405
Education and health services	2,525,900	174,989
Leisure and hospitality services	1,887,300	98,830
Other services	550,800	51,468
Information	490,300	203,521
Government	2,495,200	300,275
Trade, transportation, and utilities	2,994,700	361,192
Manufacturing	1,286,900	278,584
Finance, insurance, and real estate	809,200	525,264
Construction	765,400	87,497
Mining and natural resources	26,300	10,509
Agriculture	445,100	39,000
Total, all sectors	16,826,500	2,458,535

SOURCE: California Employment Development Department, www.labormarketinfo.edd.ca.gov/data/industries.html (accessed June 16, 2016); and U.S. Department of Commerce, Bureau of Economic Analysis, "GDP by State," www.bea.gov (accessed June 16, 2016).

of certain farm products, they achieved some improvements in working conditions, but the struggle continues today. California's agricultural industry is also caught up in environmental issues, including pesticide use and water pollution. The biggest issue, however, is always water supply. Most of California's cities and farms must import water from other parts of the state. Thanks to government subsidies, farmers claim 80 percent of the state's water supply at prices so low that they have little reason to improve inefficient irrigation systems. Meanwhile, the growth of urban areas is limited by water supplies. A drought beginning in 2012 and reaching crisis proportions in 2014 hit both farmers and city dwellers hard, with lost crops in some places and rationing or penalties for wasting water in others. Today, with agricultural and urban interests in conflict, water policy is in the forefront of California politics, as it has been so often in the past (see Chapter 10).

Agriculture is big business, but many more Californians work in manufacturing, especially in the aerospace, defense, and high-tech industries. Employment in manufacturing, however, has declined in California in recent years, especially after the federal government reduced military and defense spending in the 1990s when the collapse of communism in the Soviet Union brought an end to the Cold War. Jobs in California shifted to postindustrial occupations such as retail sales, tourism, and services, which usually pay less than manufacturing jobs did. Government policies on growth, the environment, and taxation affect all of these employment sectors, and all suffer when any one sector goes into a slump.

But the salvation of California's economy is innovation, especially in telecommunications, entertainment, medical equipment, international trade, and high-tech businesses spawned by defense and aerospace companies. By the 1990s, California hosted one-fourth of the nation's high-tech firms, which provided nearly a million jobs. Half of the nation's computer engineers worked in **Silicon Valley**, named after the silicon chip that revolutionized the computer industry. Running between San Jose and San Francisco, Silicon Valley became a center for innovation in technology from computers to software and Internet-based businesses, including iconic companies like Hewlett-Packard, Intel, Facebook, and Google, which are headquartered there. Biomedical and pharmaceutical companies also proliferated, further contributing to California's transformation. By 2016, the Silicon Valley region was leading the state and the country in job creation, but as high-tech firms expanded into San Francisco, issues of tax subsidies and gentrification arose, with affluent high-tech workers edging out local residents and driving up the price of housing there.

Computer technology also spurred expansion of the entertainment industry, long a key component of California's economy. This growth particularly benefited the Los Angeles area. Besides film and television production, tourism remains a bastion of the economy, with California ranking first among the states in visitors. Along with agriculture, high-tech, telecommunications, and other industries, these businesses have made California a leader in both international and domestic trade. All these industries are part of a globalized economy, with huge amounts of trade going through the massive port complex of Los Angeles/ Long Beach, as well as the San Francisco Bay Port of Oakland.

The California economy has been on a rollercoaster for the past few years, though. It has been in and out of recession—first in the early 1990s, and then again after the terrible events of September 11, 2001, when the California-centered Internet boom went bust as thousands of dot-com companies failed to generate projected profits. At about the same time, an energy crisis hit California; prices for gas and electricity rose, and parts of the state experienced shortages of electrical power. These factors combined to push California into another recession. Tax revenues declined precipitously, producing a huge state budget deficit. The energy crisis, the deficit, and other issues contributed to the recall of Governor Davis in 2003, but having a new governor didn't solve California's problems.

After a resurgence in 2006–2007, California's economy was hit by the Great Recession. Population growth slowed, and some Californians left. Unemployment reached 12.4 percent in 2010 (the U.S. rate at that time was 9.7 percent). Population growth slowed, and a significant number of Californians fled states with more jobs and a lower cost of living. Eventually, high-tech and Silicon Valley led the way to an economic comeback, hitting an unemployment rate of just 3.7 percent in 2016 while statewide unemployment was 5.2 percent—slightly higher than the national rate of 4.7 percent.

Throughout its history, California has experienced economic ups and downs like these, recovered, reinvented itself, and moved on, thanks to the diversity of its economy and its people and their ability to adapt to change. While some businesses have forsaken California for other states, complaining of burdensome regulation and the high cost of doing business in California, the skill and higher productivity of the state's workforce, access to capital, and quality of life compensate for such costs and keep the state attractive to many businesses.[4] Innovation continues to be an economic mainstay as well. Nanotechnology companies, for example, are concentrated in the San Francisco Bay Area, while biotechnology thrives in the San Diego region and green industry, such as solar power and electric cars, booms throughout California. Access to venture capital investment funds facilitates such innovation in California. Every year, over half of all venture capital in the United States is invested in California—especially Silicon Valley. Another strength of the California economy is an astounding and ever-growing number of small businesses—many of which are minority-owned. Most other states lack these advantages; some are dependent on a single industry or product, and none can match the energy and optimism brought by California's constant flow of immigrants eager to take jobs in the state's new and old industries.

California's globalized economy consistently attracts more immigrants than any other state, including great waves of newcomers from the 1880s to the 1920s, more during the Great Depression, and still more since the 1980s. As of 2014, 27 percent of the state's population was foreign-born, while 13 percent of the total U.S. population was from other countries. Fifty-two percent of California's immigrants are from Latin America (mostly Mexico), and 38 percent are from Asia (especially the Philippines, China, Vietnam, India, and Korea). Recently, however, immigrants from Asia have outnumbered those from Latin America. Significantly for the California economy, 80 percent of the state's immigrant population is of working age (18–64).[5] An estimated 2.7 million

T A B L E 1.3 California's Racial and Ethnic Diversity

	1990	2000	2014
Non-Latino white	57.1%	47.3%	38.8%
Latino	26.0	32.4	39.0
Asian/Pacific Islander	9.2	11.4	13.4
Black	7.1	6.5	5.8
Native American	0.6	0.5	0.4
Mixed race	N.A.	1.9	2.6

SOURCE: U.S. Census; California Department of Finance, www.dof.ca.gov (accessed June 10, 2016).

immigrants are in California illegally.[6] As a consequence of so much immigration, 44 percent of all Californians over the age of five speak a language other than English at home,[7] resulting in a major challenge for California schools. As in past centuries, immigration and language have been hot-button political issues in California in recent years.

Table 1.3 shows the extent of California's ethnic diversity. Non–Latino whites outnumbered other groups until 2014, when Latinos became the single largest group, a trend that is projected to continue. Overall, the black and white proportions of California's population have decreased, while Asian and Latino numbers have grown rapidly since the 1970s. Currently, 75 percent of students in California's public schools are nonwhite.[8]

The realization of the California dream is not shared equally among these groups. Although the median household income as of 2015 was $60,185 (U.S. median = $56,516), the income of 15.3 percent of Californians fell below the federal poverty level ($24,300 for a family of four). The rate is considerably higher when the cost of living, especially housing, is factored in. Over half the students in California schools qualify for free or reduced-price meals.[9] The gap between rich and poor in California is among the largest in the United States and is still growing. People of every race suffer from poverty in California, but it is worst among Latinos, blacks, and Southeast Asians, who tend to hold low-paying service jobs; other Asians, along with Anglos, predominate in the more comfortable professional classes.

As the poor grow in number, some observers fear that California's middle class is vanishing. Once a majority, many middle-class families have slipped down the economic ladder, and others have fled the state. Recent growth has been concentrated in low- and high-wage jobs. Many people are doing very well at the top of the ladder, but more are barely getting by at the bottom. The income gap continues to widen as California's middle class shrinks—faster than in any other state.[10]

The cost of housing is at the heart of this problem. Home prices dropped during the housing crisis of 2008–2011, briefly increasing affordability for some families, but others suffered losses of equity and some lost their homes to foreclosure. Home values in California began rising again in 2012 and hit a new median price of $509,100 in 2016, while the U.S. median was $321,100.[11] A family would need twice the median household income in California to qualify for a mortgage to purchase a home at the median price. Californians spend substantially more of their income on housing than the national average, and fewer families can afford to own homes, especially in the coastal counties from San Diego to San Francisco. Homes are more affordable in inland California, however. Overall, home ownership in California lags well behind the national average, especially for Latinos and blacks.

Access to health care has also a problem for many Californians, but the successful implementation Covered California—the state's version of the Affordable Care Act (Obamacare)—cut the percentage of residents without health insurance from 22 percent to 11 percent. Attempting to further expand coverage, the state extended Medi-Cal, an insurance program for the poor, to undocumented children in 2015 and, in 2016, applied for a waiver from the federal government to allow undocumented immigrants to purchase health insurance through Covered California.

Geographic divisions complicate California's economic and ethnic diversity.[12] In the past, the most pronounced of these divisions was between the northern and southern portions of the state. The San Francisco Bay Area tended to be diverse, liberal, and (in elections) Democratic, while southern California was staunchly Republican and much less diverse. However, with growth and greater diversity, Los Angeles also began voting Democratic. Today, the greatest division is between the coastal and inland regions of the state (see Figure 2.3). Democrats now outnumber Republicans in San Diego, and even traditionally conservative Orange County has elected a Latina Democrat to Congress.

But as the differences between northern and southern California fade, the contrast between coastal and inland California has increased. The state's vast Central Valley now leads the way in population growth, with cities from Sacramento to Fresno and Bakersfield gobbling up farmland. The Inland Empire, from Riverside to San Bernardino, has grown even more rapidly over the past quarter century. Although still sparsely populated, California's northern coast, Sierra Nevada, and southern desert regions are also growing, while retaining their own distinct identities. Water, agriculture, and the environment are major issues in all these areas. Except for Sacramento, inland California is more conservative than the coastal region of the state. Perhaps ironically, the liberal counties of the coast contribute more per capita in state taxes, and the conservative inland counties receive more per capita for social service programs.[13] While coastal California remains politically dominant, the impact of inland areas on California politics increases with every election.

These differences are such that parts of the state occasionally propose seceding, while many people lament California's underrepresentation in the U.S. Senate, where our two senators are matched by two from Wyoming with a population of less than 600,000. An initiative proposal to break California into six separate states provoked a lot of discussion in 2014, but despite $5 million spent to gather signatures, the measure failed to qualify for the ballot.

CALIFORNIA'S PEOPLE, ECONOMY, AND POLITICS

All these elements of California's economic, demographic, and geographic diversity vie with one another for political influence in the context of political structures that were created more than a hundred years ago. Dissatisfaction with this system has resulted in dozens of reforms by ballot measure, a recall election, and even calls for a constitutional convention to rewrite the state constitution entirely. Public frustration reached a nadir in 2010, when only 16 percent of Californians felt that the state was "going in the right direction," but in 2016, as the economy improved, 54 percent were optimistic about the direction of the state.[14] In the chapters that follow, we'll see how the diverse interests of our state operate in the current political system and gain an understanding of how it all works, how some changes may have improved conditions in our state, and what challenges remain.

NOTES

1. See Larry N. Gerston, *Not So Golden After All: The Rise and Fall of California*. Boca Raton: CRC Press, 2012.

2. For an overview of California history, see Kevin Starr, *California: A History*. New York: Modern Library, 2005.

3. Frank Norris, *The Octopus*. New York: Penguin, 1901. A novel of nineteenth-century California.

4. Public Policy Institute of California, "California's Future: Economy," January 2016, www.ppic.org (accessed June 10, 2016), p. 16

5. Migration Policy Institute, "State Immigration Data Profiles," www.migationpolicy .org (accessed June 11, 2016).

6. "Statistical Portrait of the Foreign-Born Population in the United States," Pew Hispanic Research Center, September 28, 2015, www.pewhispanic.org (accessed June 10, 2016).

7. "Language Use in the United States: 2013," U.S. Census, 2015, www.census.gov /data/tables/2013/demo/2009-2013-lang-tables.html (accessed June 10, 2016).

8. CalEdFacts, California Department of Education, www.cde.ca.gov (accessed June 10, 2016).

9. "Student Eligibility to Receive Free or Reduced Price Meals," www.kidsdata.org (accessed June 11, 2016).

10. 24/7 Wall St., "States Where the Middle Class Is Dying," January 22, 2015, www.247wallst.org (accessed June 11, 2016).

11. California Association of Realtors, www.car.org; and U.S. Census, www.census.gov /construction/nrs/pdf/uspricemon.pdf (accessed June 13, 2016).

12. See Richard A. Walker and Suresh K. Lodha, *The Atlas of California*. Berkeley: University of California Press, 2013.

13. Report from the Legislative Analyst's Office cited in "California's Unequal Give and Take," *San Jose Mercury News*, June 21, 2010.

14. Public Policy Institute of California, "Statewide Survey Time Trends," www.ppic.org (accessed June 15, 2016).

LEARN MORE ON THE WEB

Check out the complete California Constitution:
www.leginfo.ca.gov/const-toc.html

For population statistics on the state or your area:
www.dof.ca.gov/research/demographic
http://quickfacts.census.gov/qfd/states/06000.html

For historic images of California, including photographs, documents, newspapers, political cartoons, works of art, diaries, oral histories, advertising, and other cultural artifacts:
www.calisphere.universityofcalifornia.edu

GET INVOLVED

Choose an immigrant group from anywhere in the world and research the history of that group in California. If the group has a local advocacy organization or a festival celebrating its culture, consider volunteering and/or attending the festival to learn more about the issues affecting the group.

2

California's Political Parties and Direct Democracy

LEARNING OBJECTIVES

2.1 Understand how the Progressives reformed California's political parties.

2.2 Describe the organizational structure of California's political parties.

2.3 Analyze the impact of the top-two primary on California politics.

2.4 Comment on the possibility of California becoming a one-party state.

2.5 Compare and contrast the supporters of California's political parties.

2.6 Explain the different forms of direct democracy.

2.7 Discuss the proliferation of ballot measures in recent years.

Is California becoming a one-party state? Democrats have controlled every statewide office since 2010 and command overwhelming majorities in both houses of the state legislature. Republican presidential candidates don't bother to campaign in California because they know they can't win here.

That's far from the ideal of two-party governance in which voters have a genuine choice between parties with different ideologies and platforms and the same party does not always win. So what is a political party, and what has brought California to the current dominance of one party?

Theoretically, political parties are organizations of like-minded individuals and groups that pursue public policies based on their political ideology, offer candidates for public office, and provide the candidates with organizational and financial support and hold them accountable if they are elected. In some states, parties do all these things, but in California parties are weak as organizations and perform none of these functions effectively. History tells us why: The **Progressive** reformers intentionally weakened political parties to rid California of the railroad-dominated political machine. In doing so, they unintentionally made candidate personalities, media manipulation, and fat campaign war chests as important in elections as political parties—and sometimes more so.

But if party organizations are weak in California, how can one party dominate? Largely because of the failure of the other major party to attract enough voters to prevail. An additional post-Progressive reform, the "top-two primary" introduced in 2012, has resulted in an increasing number of general election ballots pitting two candidates of the same party against one another rather than candidates of differing parties. This has reduced competition and voters' choices, but it has also resulted in competition within the dominant party between liberals and moderates—an emerging two-party system within a single party?

The Progressives also introduced **direct democracy**. Through the initiative, referendum, and recall, California voters gained the power to make or repeal laws and to remove elected officials between elections. The reformers' intent was to empower citizens, but in practice, interest groups and politicians are more likely to use—or abuse—direct democracy.

THE PROGRESSIVE LEGACY

To challenge the dominance of the **Southern Pacific Railroad**'s political machine, Progressive reformers focused on the machine's control of party conventions, where party leaders nominated their candidates for various offices. Republican reformers scored the first breakthrough in 1908, when they succeeded in electing many antirailroad candidates to the state legislature. In 1909, the reform legislators replaced party conventions with **primary elections**, in which the registered voters of each party chose the nominees. Candidates who won their party's primary in these elections faced the nominees of other parties in **general elections** in November. By instituting this system, the reformers ended the power of the machine—and the political parties—to pick candidates.

In 1910, Progressives won the office of governor and majorities in the state legislature. They quickly introduced direct democracy to give policymaking authority to the people. They also replaced the "party column ballot"—which permitted bloc voting for all the candidates of a single party by making just one mark—with separate balloting for each office. In addition, Progressive reformers introduced **cross-filing**, which permitted candidates of one party to seek the nominations of rival parties. Finally, the Progressives instituted **nonpartisan elections**, which eliminated party labels for candidates in elections for judges and local government officials.

These changes reduced the railroad's control of the political parties, but they also sapped the strength of party organizations. By allowing the voters to circumvent an unresponsive legislature, direct democracy paved the way for interest groups to make public policy. Deletion of the party column ballot encouraged voters to cast their ballots for members of different parties for different offices (**split-ticket voting**), increasing the likelihood of a divided-party government. Cross-filing enabled candidates of one party to win the nomination of what should have been the opposing party, effectively eliminating competition. Non-partisan local elections made it difficult for the parties to groom candidates and build their organizations at the grassroots level.

In 1959, when Democrats gained control of the legislature for the first time in over forty years, they outlawed cross-filing, which had been disproportionately helpful to Republican incumbents. This marked a return to the **closed primary** in which candidates filed for nomination for their own party only.

CALIFORNIA'S POLITICAL PARTIES: SYSTEM AND SUPPORTERS

Because of the Progressive reforms, political parties in California operate under unusual constraints. Although the original reformers have long since departed, the reform mentality remains very much a part of California's political culture.

The Party System

By state law, political parties qualify to place candidates on the ballot if a number of voters equal to 1 percent of the vote in the most recent gubernatorial election sign up for the party when they register to vote; alternatively, parties can submit a petition with signatures amounting to 10 percent of that vote. Once qualified, if a party retains the registration of at least 1 percent of the voters or if at least one of its candidates for any statewide office receives 2 percent of the votes cast, that party remains qualified for the next election. By virtue of their sizes, the Democratic and Republican parties have been fixtures on the ballot almost since statehood.

Minor parties, sometimes called **third parties**, are another story. Some have been on the ballot for decades; others only briefly. In 2016, the American Independent, Green, Libertarian, and Peace and Freedom parties qualified for the ballot along with Democrats and Republicans. Breaking the hold of the two major parties is difficult, however. The Democratic and Republican candidates for governor and president typically win over 95 percent of the vote. Among the smaller parties, the Greens have elected a few city and county officials.

California voters choose their party when they **register to vote**, which, as of 2016, can be done right up to the day of the election. Beginning in 2017, citizens will be automatically registered to vote when they obtain or renew their driver's licenses (unless they opt out). Before the Great Depression, California was steadfastly Republican, but during the 1930s, a Democratic majority emerged. Since then, Democrats have dominated in voter registration (see Figure 2.1), although their proportion has declined from a peak of 60 percent of registered voters in 1942 to 44.9 percent in 2016. Republican registration has slipped to 26.0 percent, while only 4.8 percent signed up with other parties. "Independent" voters (those who designate **no party preference** when they register) hit an all-time high of 24.3 percent in 2016 (see Figure 2.2), up from just 9 percent

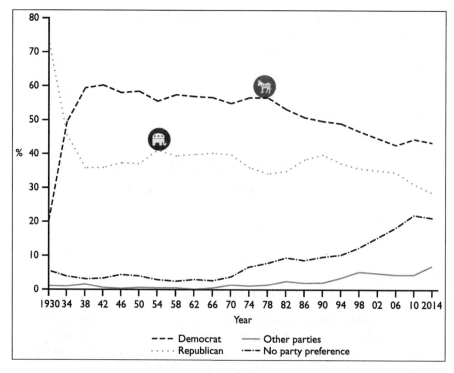

F I G U R E   2.1   Party Registration during Gubernatorial Election Years.
SOURCE: California Secretary of State.

in 1986. Despite their advantage in registration, Democrats did not gain a majority in both houses of the state legislature until 1958 and Republican candidates have won six of the last twelve gubernatorial elections.

For most of its history, California used closed primary elections to select the nominees of each party for state offices and Congress. Voters registered with a political party could cast their ballots in the primary only for that party's nominees for various offices. The winners of each party's primary election faced off in the November general election, when all voters were free to cast their ballots for the candidates of any of the parties.

But in 2010, over the strenuous objections of the political parties (another indication of their weakness), voters approved a **top-two primary** system that went into effect in 2012. In a top-two primary, no matter what their own party affiliation, voters may choose their preferred candidate from any party; the two who win the most votes face off in the November election, even if they're from the same party. Advocates of this system hoped that instead of concentrating their appeals on the core of their own parties (liberals for Democrats and conservatives for Republicans), candidates would reach out to independent and moderate voters, which would mean that those elected would be more moderate and willing to compromise when they got to Sacramento, thus reducing the likelihood of partisan gridlock.

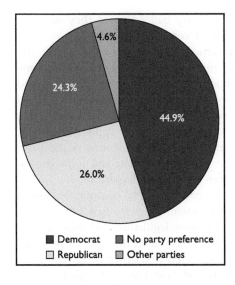

4.6%

24.3%

44.9%

26.0%

■ Democrat   ■ No party preference
☐ Republican   ■ Other parties

FIGURE 2.2 Party Registration in California, 2016. (Courtesy of Terry Christensen.)

SOURCE: California Secretary of State.

The June 2012, 2014, and 2016 elections were the first statewide top-two primaries. These elections were somewhat more competitive with more close races and more incumbent officeholders facing challengers from within their own parties than in the past. Perhaps most significantly, the top-two system resulted in twenty-eight runoffs between candidates of the same party in 2012, twenty-five in 2014, and twenty-seven in 2016, including the race for U.S. Senate. Whereas in the closed primary system, the general election choice was between the nominees of all the parties that had entered candidates in the primary, in these races voters chose between members of the same party.

In the U.S. Senate race, for example, voters in the November general election could select either Kamala Harris or Loretta Sanchez. Harris was considered more liberal and Sanchez more moderate, but both were Democrats, much to the dismay of many Republican voters, some of whom declined to vote at all in that race. Similar distinctions were common in races for the state legislature, often with traditional liberal Democrats challenged by more moderate "business" Democrats, many of whom attempted to appeal to Republican voters (as did Sanchez). Advocates of the top-two primary may be pleased that, as they hoped, more moderates have been elected to the legislature, but some voters are disappointed that they no longer have a choice between candidates of different parties while party leaders are alarmed by nasty and expensive battles within their parties. Democrats may be ascendant in California, making it virtually a one-party state, but the top-two primary has generated plenty of competition within the dominant party.

An additional impact of the top-two primary is the likely demise of the small parties. Not a single minor party candidate for legislative or statewide office has made it to the top two since the system was initiated in 2012. Surely these parties will eventually disappear under this system. Since none of the small parties secured the minimum 2 percent of the vote for one of their statewide candidates, they will appear on the next primary ballot only if they sustain a minimum registration of 1 percent of the 2014 voters.

State law dictates not only whether parties qualify for the ballot, but also party organization. The main parties have similar structures with the state **central committee** as the highest-ranking body. These committees are comprised of party candidates, officeholders, county chairpersons, and some appointed members. In addition, Democratic voters elect members from each assembly district, and Republican county central committees elect or appoint members. Each party's central committee elects a state chair who functions as the party spokesperson. Currently, Jim Brulte is the Republican chair and John Burton heads the Democrats; both are former leaders of the state legislature.

Beneath the state central committees are county central committees. Voters registered with each party choose committee members every two years during primary elections. The party's nominees for state legislature and officeholders are also members. The state and county party committees draft policy positions for party platforms, although candidates and elected officials often ignore these. Some county committees recruit volunteers and raise money for party candidates. Despite their low public profile, county committees are sometimes rife with conflict among activists. Avid liberals usually dominate Democratic county committees, whereas staunch conservatives rule Republican committees.

Party committees can endorse their preferred candidates in primary elections, which could become more important with the top-two primary system because party activists could support whichever candidate they view as most loyal. In the past, such party endorsements were rare, but both parties have endorsed more actively in recent elections. Voters don't always pay attention to such endorsements, however, and their influence is also limited by the inability of the parties to deliver organizational support to the chosen candidates and by high-spending campaigns and the media.

Party Supporters

Besides the official party organizations, many caucuses and clubs are associated with both major parties. The California Republican Assembly is a resolutely conservative statewide grassroots organization that has dominated the Republican Party, thanks to an activist membership. On the Democratic side, liberals dominate through the California Democratic Council, which comprises hundreds of local Democratic clubs organized by geography, gender, race, ethnicity, or sexual orientation.

Party activists such as these are a tiny percentage of the electorate, however. The remaining support base comes from citizens who designate their party affiliations when they register to vote and usually cast their ballots accordingly. Public opinion polls[1] tell us that voters who prefer the Democratic Party tend to be sympathetic to the poor and immigrants; concerned about health care, education, and the environment; in favor of gay rights, gun control, and abortion rights; and supportive of tax increases to provide public services. Those who prefer the Republican Party are more likely to oppose these views and to worry more about big government and high taxes. Of course, some people mix these positions.

Both major parties enjoy considerable support, but the more liberal Democratic Party fares better with blacks, city dwellers, union members, and residents of coastal California and the Sacramento area (see Figure 2.3) as well as young voters—especially Millennials. Latino voters also favor Democrats, a tendency that was strengthened by Republican support for several statewide initiatives relating to immigration and affirmative action. Voters among most Asian nationalities also lean Democratic, an inclination that has increased in recent years. As with Latinos, Asian interest in the California Republican Party has been weakened by policies and candidates perceived as anti-immigrant. The inability of Republican candidates to win support from minority voters is surely the major factor in Democratic dominance in California. More Latino and Asian voters participate every year, so unless Republicans can do more to win them over, the party may be doomed in California.

The more conservative Republican Party does better with whites, suburbanites, and rural voters, and in Orange County, the Central Valley, and inland California, as well as with older, more affluent voters, and with religious conservatives. These constituencies are more likely to turn out to vote than those that support Democrats, but some Republican leaders worry that the party has declined to such an extent that the advantage in turnout has been lost. "The California Republican Party has effectively collapsed," declared a prominent Republican political consultant. "It doesn't do any of the things that a political party should do. It doesn't register voters. It doesn't recruit candidates. It doesn't raise money.... The party is actually shrinking. It's becoming more white. It's becoming older."[2]

In the past, Republican candidates sometimes succeeded by winning the support of Democratic voters, thanks to charismatic candidates, clever campaigns, and split-ticket voting. But in the 1990s, ticket splitting declined, and instead, voters increasingly voted a straight party-line ticket—either all Democratic or all Republican. This includes no-party-preference voters, who, contrary to common wisdom, are not necessarily independent. Most tilt toward one party or the other, with Democrats enjoying greater support.[3] Some observers assert that the rightward thrust of the California's Republican Party drove independent voters to the Democrats and was even more important to Democratic dominance than was winning over minority voters.[4]

DIRECT DEMOCRACY

Thanks to the Progressives, Californians who are frustrated by the outcome of candidate elections have another way to participate in the political process. To counter the railroad machine's control of state and local governments, the Progressive reformers guaranteed the people a say through the mechanisms of direct democracy: recall, referendum, and initiative. Referenda and initiatives appear on our ballots as "propositions," with numbers assigned by the secretary of state; local measures are assigned letters by the county clerk.

FIGURE 2.3   California's Partisan Division by County, 2016. (Courtesy of Terry Christensen.)

SOURCE: California Secretary of State.

The Recall

The least-used form of direct democracy is the **recall**, which empowers voters to remove officeholders at all levels of government between scheduled elections. Advocates circulate a recall petition with a statement of their reasons for wanting a named official to be removed from office. They must collect a specific number of voter signatures within a certain time period. The numbers vary with the office in question. At the local level, for example, the number of signatures required ranges from 10 to 30 percent of those who voted in the previous local election; these signatures must be collected over periods that vary between 40 and 160 days. A recall petition for a judge or a legislator requires signatures equaling 20 percent of the vote for that office in the last election; while for state executive officeholders, the figure is 12 percent. In these cases, petitioners have 160 days to collect the signatures. If enough signatures are collected and validated by the secretary of state (for state officeholders) or by the city or county clerk (for local officeholders), an election is held. The ballot is simple: "Shall [name] be removed from the office of [title]?" The recall takes effect if a majority of voters vote yes, and then either an election or an appointment—whichever state or local law requires—fills the vacancy for the office. Elected officials who are recalled cannot be candidates in the replacement election.

Recalling state officeholders is easier in California than in the other seventeen states where recall is possible. Other states usually require more signatures, and while any reason suffices in California, other states require corruption or malfeasance by the officeholder. Nevertheless, recalls are rare in California. A dozen or so recalls are on local ballots in any given year (usually by parents angry with school board members); only about half of the officials who face recall are removed from office. Only four state legislators have been recalled. The most dramatic use of the recall came in 2003 when Governor **Gray Davis** became the first statewide official ever recalled.[5]

The Referendum

The **referendum** is another form of direct democracy, in this case allowing voters to nullify acts of the state government. Referendum advocates have ninety days after the legislature makes a law to collect a number of signatures equal to 5 percent of the votes cast for governor in the previous election (365,880 based on the 2014 vote). Referenda are even rarer than recalls. Of the fifty referenda on California ballots since 1912, voters have revoked acts of the government thirty times. In 2012, a referendum that would have repealed a redistricting plan for the state senate failed, and in 2016, a referendum to rescind a statewide ban on plastic bags was rejected despite massive campaign spending by the bag manufacturers.

The Initiative

Recalls and referenda are reactions to what elected officials do. **Initiatives** allow citizens to make policy themselves by drafting new laws or constitutional amendments and then circulating petitions to get them on the ballot. Qualifying a proposed law for a vote requires a number of signatures equal to 5 percent of the votes cast for governor in the last election; constitutional amendments require a number of signatures equal to 8 percent (585,407 based on California's 2014 election). If enough valid signatures are obtained within 180 days, the initiative goes to the voters at the next election or, on rare occasions, in a special election called by the governor. As of 2012, all citizen initiatives are on the November general election ballot only—a move advocated by Democrats because voter turnout is higher in November than in June primary elections. This means that more people participate in these decisions, but it also ensures the maximum turnout of Democratic voters.

2016 saw additional changes in the initiative process, including extending the amount of time for collecting signatures and referring initiative proposals to the legislature for consideration after petitioners collect 25 percent of the required signatures. If the legislature takes acceptable action on the initiative, its supporters can withdraw their proposal. Advocates of this change hoped it would mean more thoughtful consideration through the legislative process and, ultimately, better law. In 2016, a nasty and expensive election battle was avoided when the legislature and governor reached a compromise that satisfied the proponents of a ballot measure to raise the state's minimum wage, and the latter withdrew their initiative.

The subjects of initiatives vary wildly and are often controversial. In the past, voters have approved limits on bilingual education, banned same-sex marriage, and set standards for the size of chicken cages. Other recent propositions have dealt with gun control, requiring actors in adult films to use condoms, taxes on cigarettes, and legalizing the sale of marijuana as well as contradictory initiatives on the death penalty.

Twenty-three other states provide for the initiative, but few rely on it as heavily as California. Relatively few initiatives appeared on ballots until the 1970s, however (see Table 2.1). Then political consultants, interest groups, and politicians rediscovered the initiative, and ballot measures proliferated, peaking with eighteen initiatives on both the 1988 and 1990 election ballots. The numbers tapered off after that, but voters faced seventeen propositions in 2016—in part because the number of signatures required for a measure to qualify for the ballot was determined by voter turnout in 2014, which was historically low, thus reducing the number of signatures required and making qualifying for the ballot easier.

Legislative Initiatives, Constitutional Amendments, and Bonds

Propositions can also be placed on the ballot by the state legislature—on either the primary or general election ballots (unlike citizen initiatives). Such **legislative initiatives** can include new laws that the legislature prefers to put before the voters rather than enact on its own, or proposed **constitutional amendments**, for which voter approval is compulsory. The top-two primary measure, for example, was put on the ballot by the legislature as part of a deal to win the vote of a Republican senator for the proposed budget. In 2016, the legislature proposed and voters approved **Proposition 58**, which removed limits on bilingual education imposed by a 1998 initiative.

Voter approval is also required when the governor or the legislature seeks to issue **bonds** (borrowing money) to finance parks, schools, transportation, or other infrastructure projects. Few of these proposals are controversial, and more than 60 percent pass with minimal campaigning or spending. In 2014 (a drought year), voters approved $7.5 billion in bonds for water projects; in 2016, they consented to $9 billion in bonds for schools.

T A B L E   2.1   The Track Record of California Initiatives*

Period	Number	Number	
		Adopted	Rejected
1912–1919	31	8	23
1920–1929	34	10	24
1930–1939	37	10	27
1940–1949	20	7	13
1950–1959	11	1	10
1960–1969	10	3	7
1970–1979	24	7	17
1980–1989	53	25	28
1990–1999	61	24	37
2000–2009	60	21	39
2010–2016	31	15	16
Total	372	131 (35.2%)	241 (64.8%)

*Not including legislative initiatives.
SOURCE: California Secretary of State.

THE POLITICS OF BALLOT PROPOSITIONS

The recent proliferation of ballot propositions is hardly the result of a sudden surge in citizen action. Rather, it stems largely from the opportunism of special interests, individual politicians, and public relations firms.

Although intended as a mechanism for citizens to shape policy, even the most grassroots-driven initiative costs a million dollars to gather signatures and millions more to mount a successful campaign. "If you pay enough," declared a former chief justice of the California Supreme Court, "you can get anything on the ballot. You pay a little bit more and you get it passed."[6] The campaigns for and against the 2008 proposition banning same-sex marriage spent a total of $83 million—much of which came from out of state, because California is often seen as setting precedents for campaigns elsewhere. Health-care and insurance corporations spent over $110 million fighting consumer-oriented initiatives in 2014, and pharmaceutical companies ("big pharma") spent more than that to defeat a 2016 measure that would have required state agencies to pay the lowest prices for prescription drugs paid by the U.S. Department of Veterans Affairs. Energy, oil, and tobacco interests have also spent heavily fighting environmental- or consumer-oriented initiatives, and labor unions are big financial backers of tax measures and other initiatives that serve their interests.

Total spending for campaigns for and against propositions in any given election year averages around $300 million, but spending on the 2016 proposition campaigns, topping $500 million, broke all records. Most of this money comes from corporations, unions, and obscure political action committees (PACs), sometimes from out of state. A study by the California Fair Political Practices Commission concluded that "a handful of special interests have a disproportionate amount of influence on California elections and public policy."[7]

Wealthy individuals also use their resources to influence public policy through initiative campaigns. Business magnate Charles Munger spent tens of millions of dollars advocating redistricting reform (successfully). Tom Steyer, a hedge fund manager, spent $21.9 million supporting a 2012 initiative to close a corporate tax loophole (successfully). Facebook cofounder Sean Parker was a major supporter of the 2016 initiative to legalize marijuana to the tune of $8.6 million. Similarly, politicians use initiatives to further their own careers or shape public policy. Movie star Arnold Schwarzenegger sponsored a 2002 initiative to fund after-school programs that launched his political career. As governor, he tried to use ballot measures to further his agenda when thwarted by the Democratic majority in the legislature, but the voters rejected his efforts at political and budget reform. Governor **Jerry Brown**, on the other hand, won voter approval for his 2012 initiative to increase state revenues, although Charles Munger (see above) contributed over $35 million to the campaign against the measure. In 2016, Lieutenant Governor Gavin Newsom, perhaps to keep himself in the public eye as a candidate for governor in 2018, sponsored a successful gun control measure even though the state legislature had already passed similar laws.

Others also take advantage of direct democracy. Public relations firms and **political consultants**, virtual "guns for hire," have developed lucrative careers managing initiative and referenda campaigns; they offer expertise in public opinion polling, computer-targeted mailing, and television advertising—the staples of modern campaigns. Some firms generate initiatives themselves by conducting test mailings and preliminary polls in hopes of snagging big contracts from proposition sponsors.

Political ideology and party politics also shape the initiative wars. Stymied by Democratic dominance of the state legislature for so long, Republicans, conservatives, and business interests have, often successfully, resorted to the initiative process to pursue their agendas, especially with regard to taxes (see Chapter 8). Democrats countered in 2011 by mandating that all citizen initiatives be voted on in November, when more Democrats participate, rather than June, when lower turnout produces a more conservative electorate.

Surely the Progressive framers of direct democracy didn't intend that moneyed interests should have the advantage over the efforts of regular citizens. But direct democracy still offers hope to those out of power by enabling them to take their case to the public. Grassroots groups have won some initiative battles in recent years, including funding mental health programs by increasing taxes on the rich and regulating the treatment of farm animals, despite the strong opposition of agribusiness. The 2016 ballot included propositions addressing juvenile justice, the death penalty, an increase in cigarette taxes to fund health care, and regulations on the price of state-funded drugs. Some passed and some failed, largely due to massive spending by opponents, but they all got on the ballot largely by grassroots efforts. Such grassroots-generated measures are often defeated by well-funded opponents, but at least direct democracy provides non-elites an opportunity to make their cases.

Besides the problem of big money, the initiative process sometimes doesn't result in good laws. Because self-interested sponsors draft initiatives and media masters run campaigns, careful and rational crafting of proposals is rare. Flaws or contradictions in the laws enacted by initiative may take years to resolve, some-times in the process of implementation or through the legislative process—or by taking the issue back to the voters with successor initiatives. The recent reform that allows initiative proponents to withdraw their measures if the legislature enacts laws that meet their concerns may improve this situation by providing an oppor-tunity for more thoughtful drafting of the laws and decreasing the likelihood that they'll be challenged in the courts. Disputes about initiatives that do go to the ballot are still likely to end up in court, however, as state and federal courts are asked to rule on whether the initiatives are consistent with other laws and with the state and federal constitutions. In recent years, courts have overturned all or parts of initiatives dealing with illegal immigration, campaign finance, and same-sex marriage (see Chapter 6). Such rulings may seem to deny the will of the voters, but the electorate cannot make laws that contradict the state or federal constitutions.

The increased use of direct democracy has also had an impact on the power of our elected representatives. Although we expect them to make policy, their ability to do so has been constrained by initiatives in recent decades. This is par-ticularly the case with the state budget, much of which is dictated by past ballot measures rather than by the legislature or the governor.

The proliferation of initiatives, expensive and deceptive campaigns, flawed laws, and court interventions have annoyed voters and policy makers alike. Perhaps as a consequence, two-thirds of all initiatives are rejected (see Table 2.1). The recent reform allowing the legislature to modify and enact proposed ballot measures may result in somewhat fewer initiatives and sounder policy, but Californians still express frustration with the volume of initiatives they face and the expensive and often confusing campaigns. Opinion polls, how-ever, consistently report a solid majority in support of direct democracy—in concept.

POLITICAL PARTIES AND DIRECT DEMOCRACY

So has California become a one-party state? Voter support for the Republican Party has wilted, especially among young people, minorities, and even indepen-dents. Meanwhile, competition between the two parties has declined—most nota-bly in district or statewide contests where the top-two primary winners are of the same party. In an increasing number of races (nearly 20 percent), the final choice for voters is between a moderate or more liberal Democrat or in a few cases between a moderate or more conservative Republican—but not a choice between the two parties. And the parties, as organizations, do not have the power to control this intraparty competition. Republican candidates in California's 2016 U.S. Senate primary, for example, cumulatively won enough votes to make the top-two runoff against the top Democrat. But multiple candidates split the vote so a Democrat beat them all to the number two spot. Surely the parties will try to manage the number of candidates in future, but given their limited organizational power, they are unlikely to succeed.

All this does not make California a one-party state, however. Democrats may yet self-destruct through overconfidence or intraparty competition. And as Republican Arnold Schwarzenegger proved just a few years ago, the right Republican at the right time can win a statewide election. In 2014, a little known and minimally funded Republican challenger to popular Democratic Governor Jerry Brown scored 40 percent of the statewide vote. To increase that number, the party will need to win over young, minority, and independent voters, however, and the Republican candidate for president in 2016 may not have furthered that cause.

Genuinely competitive parties are surely better for voter choice and for democracy, but even if California becomes a one-party state, the mechanisms of direct democracy guarantee an alternative means of making policy and holding government accountable. Voters may be confounded by the proliferation of propositions and frustrated that powerful interest groups (see Chapter 4) with deep pockets so often win the initiative wars, but direct democracy still offers an engaged citizenry the opportunity to take action.

NOTES

1. Public Policy Institute of California, "California Voter and Party Profiles," *Just the Facts*, August 2015, www.ppic.org (accessed July 25, 2016).

2. Quoted in Adam Nagourney, "In California, G.O.P. Fights Steep Decline," *New York Times*, July 23, 2012.

3. Edward L. Lascher, Jr., and John L. Korey, "The Myth of the Independent Voter, California Style," *California Journal of Politics and Public Policy* 3, no. 1, 2011.

4. Morris P. Fiorina and Samuel J. Abrams, "Is California Really a Blue State?" in *The New Political Geography of California*, ed. Frederick Douzet, Thad Kousser, and Kenneth P. Miller. Berkeley: Berkeley Public Policy Press, Institute of Governmental Studies, University of California, 2008.

5. See Larry N. Gerston and Terry Christensen, *Recall! California's Political Earthquake*. Armonk: M. E. Sharpe, 2004.

6. Ronald George, "Promoting Judicial Independence," *Commonwealth*, February 2006, p. 9.

7. California Fair Political Practices Commission, *Big Money Talks: A Report*, Sacramento: California Fair Political Practices Commission, 2010.

LEARN MORE ON THE WEB

For public opinion polls, including archives:
    www.field.com/fieldpoll or "Statewide Survey," www.ppic.org

For information about California's political parties:
    American Independent Party: www.aipca.org
    California Democratic Party: www.cadem.org
    California Republican Party: www.cagop.org
    Green Party of California: www.cagreens.org
    Libertarian Party of California: www.ca.lp.org
    Peace and Freedom Party: www.peaceandfreedom.org

To find out more about elections and ballot measures:
    Ballotpedia: www.ballotpedia.org
    California Secretary of State: www.sos.ca.gov/elections
    California Voter Foundation: www.calvoter.org
    League of Women Voters: www.smartvoter.org and www.easyvoterguide.org

GET INVOLVED

Volunteer or intern for a political party by contacting your local county party offices. You'll get a chance to see what goes on in a party office and to observe the sorts of people who are active in the party you choose and their perspectives on the issues.

3

California Elections, Campaigns, and the Media

LEARNING OBJECTIVES

3.1 Examine how variation in voter participation affects election outcomes.

3.2 Compare and contrast the diversity of California candidates and population.

3.3 Discuss the roles of money and media in campaigns.

3.4 Understand the changing role of media in California politics.

D o political campaigns matter? Most of us are just annoyed by political mailers, TV ads, robocalls (recorded messages), tweets, and Facebook posts. But how else can we learn about candidates and ballot measures? A typical California ballot requires voters to make decisions about over twenty elective positions and propositions. Even the best-informed citizens find it difficult to choose among candidates for offices they know little about and to decide on obscure and complicated propositions. Political party labels provide some guidance, but with the **top-two primary**, voters must choose between candidates of the same party with increasing frequency.

Like them or not, campaigns, along with the news media, are important sources of information for California voters—and the media and campaigns together are crucial in California elections. The mobility that characterizes California society enhances their influence. Nearly half of all Californians were born elsewhere, and many voters in every California state election are participating for the first time. Residents also move frequently within the state, reducing the political influence of families, friends, and peer groups and boosting that of campaigns and the media.

THE VOTERS

California citizens who are eighteen years or older are eligible to vote unless they are convicted felons in prison or on parole or in mental institutions. Those eligible must **register to vote** by completing a form available at post offices, libraries, and other public places or online at registertovote.ca.gov. Under California's new "motor voter" law, citizens will be automatically registered to vote when they obtain or renew their driver's licenses (unless they opt out) beginning in 2017.

Altogether, nearly 24.8 million Californians are eligible to vote. Only 19.4 million (78 percent) were registered in 2016, however, and many of those who are registered don't vote. In the gubernatorial election of 2014, only 42.2 percent of registered voters participated. Turnout is higher in presidential elections, which are held in even-numbered years, alternating with gubernatorial elections. In 2016, 75.3 percent of the state's registered voters participated in the presidential election. Far fewer voters participate in June primary elections, however—47.7 percent in the 2016 presidential primary and 25.2 percent in the 2014 gubernatorial primary (see Figure 3.1).

Traditionally, voters go to designated precinct (or neighborhood) polling places to cast their ballots, but over the years, more and more Californians have opted to **vote by mail** because it's so much more convenient (see Figure 3.2). Voters sign up to do so when they register to vote, and then ballots are automatically sent to them for every election. All they have to do is complete their ballots and get them in the mail before the election or drop them off at their precinct polling place on Election Day.

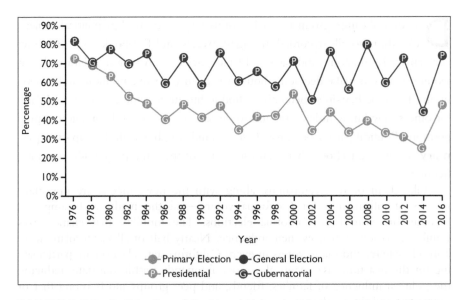

FIGURE 3.1 Participation of Registered Voters in Primary and General Elections, 1976–2016.

SOURCE: California Secretary of State.

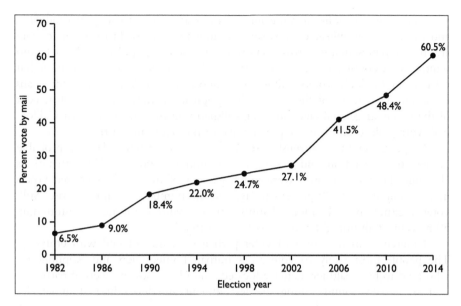

FIGURE 3.2 Voting by Mail in California's Gubernatorial Elections.
SOURCE: California Secretary of State.

Besides the convenience of voting by mail, many people prefer to deal with California's complex ballots at their leisure, and, increasingly, campaigns push identified supporters to vote by mail to ensure their participation. With many more people voting by mail—up to three weeks before Election Day—campaigns have had to change tactics. Rather than a big push in the last few days before the election, they must spread their resources over a longer period.

Voting by mail and easier registration may have increased voter participation slightly, and the new "motor voter" policy is expected to add two million more registered voters in 2017 alone,[1] but despite making registration and voting easier than most other states, voter participation in California ranked forty-third among the fifty states in 2014 and forty-second in 2012.[2] Why do so many Californians choose not to vote? Some still aren't registered, but millions who are registered nevertheless do not vote. Some are apathetic, some are unaware, and some feel uninformed. Others are cynical about politics and politicians. Most commonly, nonvoters say they're just not interested in politics or they're too busy.[3] Some say election information is too hard to understand, and others are bewildered by all the messages that bombard them during a typical California election.

Could voter turnout in California be improved? Registration can't be made much easier, but voting could be made more convenient by changing Election Day from Tuesday or voting entirely by mail like some other states and recently some California counties. Although ballots are already available in many languages, simplifying their content (in any language) could also help. Perhaps better civic education is needed, too. Better news coverage might also stimulate turnout and so would campaigns that inspire rather than alienate voters.

The efforts of political campaigns to motivate voters to support candidates and causes are complicated, however, because those who do turn out to vote are not a representative cross section of the actual population. Non-Latino whites, for example, make up 42 percent of California's adult population but 60 percent of likely voters. Although Latinos, African Americans, and Asians constitute 58 percent of the state's adult population, they are only 40 percent of the voters in general elections.[4] This disparity in turnout means that California's voting electorate is not representative of the state's population.

Language, culture, citizenship status, and socioeconomic class are probable barriers to registration and voting among minority groups. This situation is changing, however. Latinos were just 8 percent of the state's registered voters in 1978 but are over 20 percent today, and the number continues to rise. Still, voter registration lags among Latino citizens, who comprise an astounding 59 percent of all unregistered voters in California.[5]

Differences in the levels of voter participation do not end with ethnicity. The people most likely to vote are suburban homeowners and Republicans, who tend to be wealthier, better educated, and older. Lower levels of participation are usually found among the less affluent and less educated, inner-city residents, the young, and Democrats.

According to recent reports, 48 percent of likely voters in California are over the age of fifty-five, although this group is 31 percent of the state population, while adults aged eighteen to thirty-four are 33 percent of the population and only 18 percent of likely voters.[6] All this adds up to a voting electorate that is more conservative than the population as a whole, which explains how Republicans sometimes win statewide elections despite the Democratic edge in registration and why liberal ballot measures often fail.

Of course, voting is only one form of political participation. Many people sign petitions, attend public meetings, write letters or e-mails to officials, and contribute money to campaigns. A recent report, however, found that California lags behind other states in "non-electoral civic engagement."[7] As with voting, those who participate most are white, older, more affluent, homeowners, and more highly educated. Does the differential in voting and other forms of participation matter? It seems self-evident that elected officials pay more attention to the concerns of those who participate than those who do not.

THE CANDIDATES

When we vote, we choose among candidates, but where do candidates come from? Some are encouraged to run by political parties or interest groups seeking to advance their causes. Political leaders looking for allies recruit others, although weak political parties make such overtures less common in California than elsewhere. The wide-open nature of the top-two primary—also called the "jungle primary"—further weakens the prospects of candidate recruitment by the political parties. In fact, many candidates are self-starters with an interest in politics who just decide to run and then seek support. The rising cost and increasing negativity of campaigns have discouraged some people from running, although wealthy individuals who can fund their own campaigns have offered themselves as candidates in recent years. Most candidates start at the bottom of the political ladder, running for school board or city council, and work their way up, building support as they go. Others gain experience as staff members for elected officials, eventually running for their boss's job. Wealthy candidates sometimes skip such apprenticeships and run directly for higher office, but the voters are often skeptical because of their lack of political experience.

Historically, candidates in California have been even less representative of the population than the electorate. Most have been educated white males of above-average financial means. The 1990s brought change, however. Underrepresented groups such as women, racial and ethnic minorities, and gay men and lesbians grew in strength and organization, and structural changes facilitated their candidacies. **Term limits** restricting the number of times legislators could be reelected were introduced, thus ensuring greater turnover in the state legislature. In addition, **redistricting** after the censuses of 1990, 2000, and 2010 resulted in redrawn legislative and congressional districts that gave minority candidates new opportunities.

These changes resulted in a surge of successful women and Latino candidates for the state legislature and Congress (see Chapter 5, Figure 5.3). Many women and Latino candidates have also been elected as county supervisors, city council members, mayors, and school board members. Although they form a smaller minority, African Americans gained a foothold in state politics earlier than Latinos, electing state legislators and winning statewide office, but black representation has shrunk as that of other minorities has increased and the state's African American population has not grown proportionately. However, California's new U.S. senator, Kamala Harris, is African American, Asian, and Native American. Asian Americans are currently the most underrepresented of California's racial minorities, although two statewide offices (treasurer and controller) are currently held by Asian Americans and seventeen are members of the state legislature. Electing candidates has been challenging for Asian Americans because many are recent immigrants who are not yet rooted in the state's political system and because there are cultural and political differences among the Chinese, Japanese, Vietnamese, Koreans, Indo-Americans, and others. But like women and Latinos, these groups generate more candidates in every election and many Asians now serve on city councils and school boards.

Lesbians and gay men achieved elected office later than any of these groups. Greater bias may be a factor, and in the past, the closeted status of homosexual candidates and elected officials weakened organizing efforts and made gay and lesbian elective successes invisible. Nevertheless, over 100 openly gay and lesbian individuals have won election to local offices and as judges, and eight serve in the state legislature.

Despite recent electoral successes, all these groups remain underrepresented partly because of racism and sexism but also because many members of these groups are economically disadvantaged, which makes it hard to participate in politics, let alone to take on the demands of a candidacy. Women, minorities, and gay men and lesbians are usually not plugged in to the network of lobbyists, interest groups, and big donors that provide funds for California's expensive campaigns. Minorities also have difficulty winning support outside their own groups and may alienate their natural constituencies in the process. The fact that minorities are less likely to vote than whites further reduces their candidates' potential. Nevertheless, when someone from any of these groups becomes a candidate, members of the group are excited to see one of their own running and voter participation within the group increases. Recently, for example, Vietnamese candidates have galvanized their communities, and several have won public office. Meanwhile, organizations within each of these constituencies recruit, train, and support candidates, and the diversity of California candidates and elected officials increases with each election.

THE MONEY

The introduction of primary elections in 1909 shifted the focus of campaigns from political parties to individual candidates, and the introduction of the top-two primary in 2010 reinforced that trend. Thanks to these reforms in candidate selection, California's political parties have little or no control over who their candidates will be; and because the parties also contribute little money or staff, political aspirants must raise money, recruit workers, research issues, and plot strategy on their own—or with the help of expensive consultants.

Without significant help from the parties, candidates must promote themselves, and the cost of running for state assembly or senate often exceeds $1 million. Campaigns for statewide offices are even more expensive. Over $254 million was spent on the race for governor in 2010, although much less was spent in 2014 because Governor **Jerry Brown** was an overwhelming favorite to win reelection. Spending on races for all candidates for the legislature totaled over $135 million in the 2013–2014 election cycle.[8]

Interest groups, businesses, and wealthy individuals provide the money. Much campaign financing is provided by **political action committees (PACs)**, which interest groups use to direct money to preferred campaigns. For a list of the top organizational donors, see Table 4.1 in Chapter 4. Legislative leaders such as the speaker of the assembly and the president pro tem of the senate also raise huge sums from such sources and channel the money to their allies; individual candidates raise money by directly asking potential contributors for donations and by organizing special fundraising events, which range from barbecues to banquets and concerts. They also solicit contributions through targeted mailings and the Internet. Some wealthy candidates finance their own campaigns. Republican Meg Whitman broke state and national records by spending $142 million of her own money on her campaign for governor in 2010. Voters are skeptical about wealthy candidates who finance their own campaigns, however. Most such candidates, including Whitman, have lost.

Concerned about the influence of money and turned off by campaign advertising, Californians have approved a series of initiatives aimed at regulating campaign finance. The **Political Reform Act of 1974** required public disclosure

T A B L E 3.1   Proposition 34 Limits on Contributions to State Candidates, 2015–2016

Contributor	Legislature	Statewide, except Governor	Governor
Person	$4,200	$ 7,000	$28,200
Small contributor committee	$8,500	$14,100	$28,200
Political party	No limit	No limit	No limit

SOURCE: California Fair Political Practices Commission, www.fppc.ca.gov.

T A B L E 3.2   Voluntary Expenditure Ceilings for Candidates for State Offices, 2013–2016

Office	Primary	General Election
Assembly	$564,000	$987,000
Senate	846,000	1,269,000
Governor	8,460,000	14,100,000
Other statewide offices	5,640,000	8,460,000

SOURCE: California Fair Political Practices Commission, www.fppc.ca.gov.

of all donors and expenditures through the **Fair Political Practices Commission (FPPC)**. In 2000, voters approved **Proposition 34**, a legislative initiative setting contribution limits for individuals and committees (see Table 3.1).

Proposition 34 also set voluntary spending limits for candidates (see Table 3.2). Those who accept the limits have their photo and candidate statements published in the official ballot booklets that go to all voters; candidates who decline the limits are excluded from the booklet. Most candidates for the legislature and statewide offices other than governor comply with the spending limits; those who do not lose the moral high ground to those who do, which may influence some voters. There is no limit, however, on how much a candidate can contribute to his or her own campaign, which enables wealthy candidates to substantially fund their own campaigns.

Like most reforms, Proposition 34 has had unintended consequences. Money is given to political parties to spend on behalf of candidates rather than to the candidates themselves. In 2014, the Democratic Party spent $22.6 million while the Republican Party raised $19.3 million. More significantly, the new spending limits have been subverted by **independent expenditures** by PACs or groups specially organized by political consultants in support of candidates. Independent spending topped over $45 million for candidates in the competitive race for governor in 2010 and over $78 million in the 2014 legislative campaigns. Top independent expenditure groups include the Chamber of Commerce, teachers' and other unions, charter school advocates, oil companies, and hospitals.[9] In the past, union money went to Democrats while most business contributors focused on Republicans, but now with Republicans reduced to what may be a long-term minority in the legislature, business interests and others that would normally contribute to Republicans have begun taking advantage of the top-two primary to support moderate or "business" Democrats running against more traditional liberal, union-friendly Democrats in the expectation that these moderates will be more sympathetic to their interests. In 2016, independent expenditures by special interest groups topped $22 million in sixteen runoff elections between Democrats running for the state legislature.[10]

Some of this money is directly contributed to candidates, but even more is spent through independent committees supporting the candidates; and in some campaigns, independent expenditures exceed those of the candidates. The increase in such spending was accelerated with the U.S. Supreme Court's 2010 *Citizens United* decision that the First Amendment prohibited government limits on independent expenditures by unions and corporations. The only restriction on independent expenditures is that they cannot be coordinated with the campaigns of the candidates they support. Because they are not directly associated with the candidates, "independent" mailings and television ads often feature the most vicious attacks on opponents. In some races, independent expenditures exceed candidate spending, and the advertising from such expenditures communicates more with the voters than the candidates do—and not always in ways the candidates appreciate.

The latest means by which elected officials try to get around limits on direct contributions to their campaigns and yet keep control of spending of funds they raise is the "ballot measure committee." The stated purpose of these committees is to support or oppose initiatives, and dozens of such committees, controlled by elected officials, have been created in recent years. Contributions are not restricted, and most of the money comes from special interests and is spent on consultants, polling, fundraising, travel, and lawyers, not on direct support or opposition to ballot measures.[11]

Tracking campaign spending—to "follow the money"—has become ever more complex and difficult due to independent expenditures, ballot measure committees, PACs with names that cloak their real purpose and backers (the "Coalition to Restore California's Middle Class" is entirely funded by Chevron), and PACs that contribute to other PACs to obscure the individuals and interests who are actually funding campaigns. Proposition 34 regulations have been condemned as "ineffective" and even cynically deceptive "reforms."[12] Meanwhile, groups like Common Cause continue to seek ways to limit the role of money in politics.

CAMPAIGNING CALIFORNIA STYLE

Campaign contributors hope to elect allies who will support their interests, and they expect their money to buy ready access and long-term influence.

Candidates deny making specific deals, however, insisting that they and their contributors merely share views on key issues. Millions of dollars flow into candidates' coffers through this murky relationship—and still more is spent by "independent" PACs supporting candidates deemed sympathetic to their causes.

So much money is needed because California campaigns, whether local or statewide, are highly professionalized. Unable to count on the political parties for funds and support, candidates hire political consultants to recruit workers, raise money, conduct public opinion polls, design advertising, and perform virtually all other campaign activities. These specialists understand the behavior of California voters and use their knowledge to their candidate's benefit.

Costly campaigns run by professional consultants date back to the 1934 election, when the state's conservative powers, including movie studios and newspapers, spent $10 million (then a record) on a vicious campaign to defeat Upton Sinclair, a socialist who had won the Democratic nomination for governor.[13] Eighty years later in the low-turnout 2014 statewide election, campaign consultants collected over $300 million in fees for all candidates and ballot measures combined.[14]

Political consultants became indispensable with the advent of television, which allowed candidates instant entry into voters' homes and enabled them to put their messages across at the exact moment of their choosing—on broadcast or cable TV, between football games, and during the local news or *Ellen*, depending on the target audience. Unknown candidates like eBay billionaire Meg Whitman, the 2010 Republican candidate for governor, have become major contenders via massive television ad campaigns, but it's costly. A statewide TV advertising buy costs over $1 million—and one round of ads is never enough.

More than in smaller, more compact states where people are more connected, Californians rely heavily on television for political information. Television advertising is the only way to reach the mass of voters in such a big state. At the height of the campaigns, candidates run hundreds of ads a day in California's major media markets. Well-funded initiative campaigns also rely almost exclusively on television advertising, sometimes very effectively. In 2016, an initiative to regulate the price of prescription drugs was supported by the public until pharmaceutical companies poured $110 million into a confusing and deceptive television ad campaign that ultimately defeated the measure.

Television is too costly for most candidates for legislative and local offices, however. A one-time thirty-second prime-time spot costs over $20,000 in Los Angeles, and because most television stations broadcast to audiences much larger than a legislative district, the message is wasted on many viewers. Advertising during the day or on cable is cheaper, however, and many legislative candidates and PACs have turned to these alternatives. Most, however, have found a more efficient way to spend their money: **direct mail**.

Experts in direct mail develop lists of voters and their characteristics and then send special mailings to people who share particular qualities. In addition to listing voters by party registration and residence, these experts compile data identifying various groups, including liberals and conservatives, ethnic voters, retired people, homeowners and renters, union members, women, LGBT (lesbian, gay, bisexual, and transgendered) voters, and those most likely to vote. Consultants mine data on consumer interests that might predict the political or policy concerns of voters so their mailings can be microtargeted. Once the targets have been identified, campaign strategists can develop just the right message to send to them. Conservatives may be told of the candidate's opposition to taxes; liberals may be promised action on the environment. For the price of a single thirty-second television spot, local or legislative candidates can send multiple mailings to their selected audiences.

Television and direct mail dominate California campaigns because they reach the most voters and most of the money candidates and PACs raise is spent on these media, but their use is not without problems. Because television and direct mail are expensive, campaign costs have risen, as has the influence of major donors and PACs. Candidates who are unable to raise vast sums of money are usually left at the starting gate—like the Republican who ran against Jerry Brown for governor in 2014. Incumbent officeholders, who are masters at fundraising and are well connected to major contributors, become invincible.

Furthermore, these media are criticized for oversimplifying issues and emphasizing the negative. Television commercials for ballot measures reduce complicated issues to emotional thirty-second spots aimed at uninformed voters. Candidates' ads and mailings indulge in the same oversimplification, sometimes in the form of attacks on opponents, although such attacks (or "hit pieces") more often come from obscurely named independent expenditure committees these days. Voters have grown skeptical of such attacks, yet they are hard to resist; campaign consultants are certain that the public pays more attention to negative messages than to positive ones, but such negative campaigning surely increases voter cynicism and probably drives down voter participation.

Candidates and PACs also take their campaigns to the Internet, using websites and social media to communicate with and mobilize supporters, recruit volunteers, and raise money. The political impact of Internet campaigning is unclear, however. Whereas television and mail enable candidates to reach us whether we're interested or not, the voters themselves must usually initiate contact on the Internet, which limits the audience to those who are already engaged. Using social media is mostly free, however, so it's a cheap, quick, and easy way to communicate with voters—and even advertising is relatively cheap online. As with direct mail, campaigns target online ads to individual voters by collecting data about our use of email and the websites we visit. In California's 2014 election, campaigns spent only $4.3 million (5.5 percent of total spending)[15] on social media, but they probably got more bang for the buck than with other media—and with every election, they find new ways to use social media to reach and motivate voters.

Overall, California's media-oriented campaigns reinforce both the emphasis on candidates' personalities and voter cynicism. Some people blame such campaigns for declining **voter turnout**. Contemporary campaigns may also depress voter turnout by aiming all their efforts at regular voters and ignoring those who are less likely to vote—particularly minority or young voters. Although this is a sensible way to use campaign resources, it does nothing to stimulate democracy.

Some campaigns still use tried-and-true door-to-door or telephone campaigns and get-out-the-vote drives on Election Day—people actually talking to people! Labor union volunteers are a force in elections in Los Angeles and San Jose, for example, and the political parties sometimes organize volunteers to turn out voters for their candidates. Grassroots campaigns have a long and honorable tradition in California, but even in small-scale, local races, they are often up against not only big-money opponents but also the California lifestyle: few people are at home to be contacted, and those who are may let calls go to voicemail or be mistrustful of strangers at their door. Lately, however, campaigns have been asking volunteers to send messages to their friends and acquaintances by social media. Receiving a personal message from someone you know is an extremely effective (and cheap) means of persuasion. Still, candidates need money for their campaigns; those with the most money don't always win, but those with too little rarely even become contenders.

THE NEWS MEDIA AND CALIFORNIA POLITICS

From candidates and campaigns to public policy, most of what Californians know about politics—which is not necessarily very much—comes from the news media. They have a profound impact on ideas, issues, and leaders. Until the 1950s, a few family-owned newspapers dominated the media. Then television gave the newspapers some competition while expanding the cumulative clout of the mass media. Today, new online media and a plethora of ethnic publications also are contributors.

Paper Politics

California's once-great newspapers were founded in the nineteenth century by ambitious men such as Harrison Gray Otis of the *Los Angeles Times*, William Randolph Hearst of the *San Francisco Examiner*, and James McClatchy of the *Sacramento Bee*. These print-media moguls used their newspapers to boost their communities, their political candidates, and their favored causes. Most were like Otis, an ardent conservative who fought labor unions and pushed for growth while making a fortune in land investments. His *Los Angeles Times* supported the Southern Pacific Railroad's political machine and condemned Progressive leader **Hiram Johnson** as a demagogue, as did many other newspapers in the state. Other journalists, however, were at the forefront of the Progressive reform movement.

The Progressives' triumph over the machine did not diminish the influence of the newspapers. In Los Angeles, San Francisco, Oakland, San Jose, and San Diego, Republican publishers used the power of the press—in editorials and in news articles—to promote their favorite candidates and causes, helping to keep Republicans in office long after the Democrats gained a majority of registered voters.

Change came in the 1970s, when most of California's family-owned newspapers became part of corporate chains. The new managers brought in more professional editors and reporters. News coverage became more objective, and opinion was more consistently confined to the editorial pages, which became somewhat less conservative. Newspapers probably peaked in quality and influence in the 1980s, but they've been in decline since then.

California once had hundreds of newspapers, with several competing with one another in the larger cities. Today, less than 100 survive, and most cities have just one. In the Bay Area, the *San Francisco Chronicle* stands alone, while the Bay Area News Group (BANG) includes the Oakland and San Jose newspapers, nine other daily newspapers, and twenty-seven weeklies that share production facilities as well as staff and content. But the reduction and consolidation of newspapers are not the only changes. As a result of the loss of readers and advertisers to other media, the surviving newspapers have shrunk in both news coverage and staffing. The *Los Angeles Times*, for example, employs less than half as many journalists as it did in the 1990s. As a consequence, newspapers provide much less coverage of state politics than they once did. Most no longer have their own reporters in Sacramento, relying instead on the Associated Press or the Sacramento bureau of the *Los Angeles Times* for news from the Capitol.

Although they have fewer readers now, especially among young people, newspapers remain influential through what they choose to cover and through editorials expressing the opinions of publishers and journalists on their editorial boards. Some voters follow editorial recommendations on candidates and issues for lack of alternative sources of advice, especially on lower profile races and ballot measures. Nevertheless, today's newspapers are less influential than they once were as their number and readership have declined. Other media, including television and the Internet, have become more important to many people.

Television Politics

Where do you get your news about California politics? According to public opinion surveys, only 10 percent of California voters say they get most of their news and information from newspapers, with 9 percent citing radio, 32 percent the Internet (including 51 percent of younger adults), and 38 percent television.[16] But television coverage of California politics leaves a lot to be desired.

Television stations do not operate news bureaus in the state Capitol, and television news editors generally avoid state political coverage because they believe viewers want big national stories or local features, so only a tiny percentage of newscast time is devoted to state politics. Even candidates for governor have a hard time making local news broadcasts, and most television stations decline to broadcast state candidate debates out of fear of low ratings. Critics point out that if television doesn't provide news coverage, candidates are forced to buy advertising time—on television. As a consequence, candidate ads take up more time than news coverage of campaigns during the nightly news on California television stations in election years—and provide a major source of revenue for the stations. Although television reporting on state politics can be minimal and superficial, coverage has improved somewhat in the twenty-first century with the advent of transmission by satellite vans, which makes it easier for television stations to send reporters to cover breaking news and major events "live from the capital!" without the necessity of investing in permanent Sacramento bureaus.

Californians who prefer their politics raw—without reporters or commentary—can watch their government in action on the California Channel online (www .calchannel.com) or on most cable systems.

New Media

Traditional print and broadcast media still dominate, but in recent years, alternative sources of news and information have become available to Californians. Hundreds of ethnic broadcasting outlets and publications now serve Californians in Spanish, Vietnamese, Mandarin, and many other languages. Latino newspapers and television and radio stations reach major audiences, especially in southern California. Many of these ethnic media are virtually obsessed with politics as their communities generate candidates or factional conflict.

Talk radio has also become a political fixture, especially in a state where people spend so much time in their cars. Politics is a hot topic on talk radio, which played a crucial role in stirring up the recall of Governor Gray Davis in 2003.

But the medium with the most spectacular recent impact on politics is the Internet. Access to news and information on the Internet has given us exponentially more sources of information and has diverted audiences and advertisers from more traditional media, especially newspapers. Thousands of websites focus on state or local politics and give citizens direct access to their governments. Blogs by political junkies offer news and opinion and often break stories. Social media keep members of traditional interest groups in touch with one another and create whole new communities. Eighty-four percent of California households have access to the Internet, and the same percentage claim that they regularly use the Internet to follow the news—and it's the dominant source of news for younger adults. Access is not equally distributed, however. Latinos, elders, and lower income residents are less likely to have access to computers or to use the Internet.[17]

ELECTIONS, CAMPAIGNS, AND THE MEDIA

The influence of money and the media is greater in California politics than in most other states. Candidates must organize their own campaigns, raise vast sums of money, and then take their cases to the people by mail and television. Such campaigns are inevitably personality-oriented, with substantive issues taking a back seat to puff pieces or attacks on opponents. The media provide a check of sorts, but declining coverage limits their impact.

All of this takes us back to the issue of waning voter turnout. More people vote in presidential elections, but turnout in primaries and nonpresidential elections is low. Easier voter registration and the option of voting by mail haven't significantly changed this—yet. Could stronger parties, more news coverage, and more substantive, issue-oriented campaigns revive voter interest? Maybe, but campaign consultants and the media say they're already giving the public what it wants.

NOTES

1. Public Policy Institute of California, "What to Expect from California's New Motor Voter Law," June 2016, www.ppic.org (accessed August 3, 2016).

2. FairVote, "Voter Turnout," www.fairvote.org (accessed August 3, 2016).

3. Public Policy Institute of California, "Voter Participation in California," *Just the Facts*, September 2015, www.ppic.org (accessed August 3, 2016).

4. Public Policy Institute of California, "California's Exclusive Electorate," March 2016, www.ppic.org (accessed August 4, 2016).

5. *Ibid.*

6. Public Policy Institute of California, "California's Likely Voters," *Just the Facts*, September 2016, www.ppic.org (accessed October 1, 2016).

7. James E. Prieger and Kelly M. Faltis, "Non-Electoral Civic Engagement in California," *California Journal of Politics and Policy*, May 2013.

8. National Institute on Money in Politics, "California 2014," www.followthemoney.org (accessed August 5, 2016).

9. *Ibid.*

10. "In Sacramento, Industries Turn to 'Mod Squad'," *San Jose Mercury News*, September 27, 2015, and "Dems Duel Dems Across State," *San Jose Mercury News*, November 7, 2016.

11. "The New 'Slush Funds,'" *San Jose Mercury News*, August 21, 2016.

12. Dan Walters, "Proposition 34 Only Gave the Appearance of Reform," *San Jose Mercury News*, June 6, 2010.

13. See Greg Mitchell, *The Campaign of the Century: Upton Sinclair's Race for Governor of California and the Birth of Media Politics*. New York: Random House, 1992.

14. "Ho Hum California Election Cycle Paid Off for Political World," *Sacramento Bee*, March 15, 2015.

15. Maplight, "California Independent Expenditures," www.Maplight.org (accessed August 6, 2016).

16. Public Policy Institute of California, "Californians' News and Information Sources," *Just the Facts*, October 2014, www.ppic.org (accessed August 7, 2016).

17. The Field Poll, Release #2545, August 1, 2016, http://www.field.com/fieldpoll online/subscribers/2016-Digital-Divide-Special-Release.pdf (accessed November 4, 2016).

LEARN MORE ON THE WEB

For polling data about voters:
    Field Poll: http://field.com/fieldpollonline/subscribers
    Public Policy Institute of California: www.ppic.org

For information on registration, elections, and voting:
    California Secretary of State: www.sos.ca.gov
    California Voter Foundation: www.calvoter.org

Official Voter Information Guide: http://voterguide.sos.ca.gov
Voter's Edge California: www.votersedge.org/ca

To follow the money:
California Fair Political Practices Commission: www.fppc.ca.gov
Maplight: http://maplight.org
National Institute on Money in State Politics: www.followthemoney.org

News on state politics, campaigns, and elections:
California Report (radio): www.californiareport.org
Capitol Weekly: www.capitolweekly.net
Rough & Tumble: www.rtumble.com

GET INVOLVED

Register to vote online at registertovote.ca.gov. To learn how campaigns try to reach voters, volunteer or intern for a candidate in your area. You can search for candidates online with www.aroundthecapitol.com or www.votersedge.org/ca.

4

Interest Groups: The Power behind the Dome

LEARNING OBJECTIVES

4.1 Trace the evolution of group power in California.

4.2 Classify the types of interest groups.

4.3 Organize interest groups in terms of their techniques and targets.

4.4 Describe regulating groups.

4.5 Assess group clout: money, numbers, and credibility.

Many people condemn interest groups as self-serving enemies of democracy for their seemingly narrowness of purpose. But in fact, most of us—knowingly or otherwise—belong to or are affected by interest groups. How do we reconcile this conundrum? Perhaps by beginning with an explanation of these organizations. **Interest groups** protect and promote the shared political objectives of their members. Existing in all shapes and sizes, they range from labor unions, ethnic organizations, and business federations to student associations, environmental champions, and automobile clubs. Whatever their differences, interest groups seek to influence the actions of public policy makers. Sometimes, they are referred to as "special interests" for the special attention they seek and sometimes receive. Special or not, most of us are connected with one or more of these entities.

In California, interest groups have prospered and proliferated, and in some ways they have become more important than traditional political parties (see Chapter 2). That's because weak political parties and the state's election system provide a fertile political environment for organized groups to exercise influence. Candidates are often dependent upon groups for campaign contributions, while direct democracy often enables groups to take their issues directly to the voters, circumventing the legislature and other elected policy makers.

Besides exercising their influence through campaign assistance and direct democracy, interest groups also influence legislators in the hallways beneath the capitol dome. Some observers view these efforts as assisting the legislative process; others see them as manipulating that process. Either way, interest groups can be powerful forces in the policy-making arena.

THE EVOLUTION OF GROUP POWER IN CALIFORNIA

Interest group influence is found throughout California's lengthy constitution. In other states, groups gain advantages such as tax exemptions through acts of the legislature, which can be changed at any time. In California, such protections are often written into the constitution, making alteration difficult because constitutional amendments require the approval of the electorate. For example, in Article XIII, forest trees are exempt from taxation until they are forty years old; in the same Article, the tax rate for insurers is set at 2.25 percent. Only the voters can change these provisions and thousands of others.

Different interests have benefited throughout California's colorful history. In the early days, the mining industry and ranchers dominated the state's policy-making environment. From about 1870 to 1910, the Southern Pacific Railroad monopolized California's economy and politics, with incredible control over both of California's major political parties in the state legislature. Land development, shipping, and horse-racing interests next dominated the political landscape through the mid-twentieth century, followed by the automobile and defense industries. Agricultural interests have remained strong throughout the state's history.

These days, banking and service businesses tower over manufacturing, while high-tech industries have surpassed defense and aerospace. Insurance companies, teachers' associations, public safety organizations, physicians' and attorneys' groups, and other vocation-related associations also routinely lobby state government. Agribusiness remains influential, particularly with respect to water policy and land use. Organized labor and business interests—almost always at odds—continue to battle for preeminence with the legislature and voters. Public interest groups, such as the League of Women Voters, Common Cause, and The Utility Reform Network (TURN), are also part of the ever-growing interest group mix.

When elections include statewide ballot propositions, groups concerned about the outcome flood the political process with campaign funds. The 2016 general election ballot contained seventeen propositions, which led to groups (and some individuals) spending more than $500 million in their efforts to sway the public. Ballot proposals concerning more taxes, pharmaceutical purchases, prison-sentencing procedures, and firearms regulations were among those that attracted the attention of interest groups.

When the legislature is in session, interest groups are active with financial contributions as well as voluminous information for legislators, their staff members, and bureaucrats—in short, anyone who might play a role in resolving their issues. Pressured by these many organizations and their monetary offerings, California politicians often find themselves responding to the demands of the most powerful interest groups rather than governing them.

TYPES OF GROUPS

Interest groups vary in size, resources, and goals. At one extreme, groups with narrow and targeted economic benefits tend to have relatively small memberships but substantial financial resources. At the other end of the spectrum, public interest groups with large memberships tend to have little money. A few, such as the Consumer Attorneys of California (CAC), whose membership consists of 3,000 trial lawyers, have the dual advantage of being both large and well funded. Others, such as the Consumers for Auto Reliability and Safety (CARS), operate on a shoestring. Still others, such as the California Teachers Association and California Chamber of Commerce, have more members paying dues than the state Democratic and Republican parties.

Economic Groups

Economic groups that seek various financial gains or hope to prevent losses dominate the state's interest group environment. Every major corporation in the state, from Southern California Edison to the California Northern Railroad, is represented in Sacramento either by its own lobbyists or by lobbying firms hired to present the corporation's cases to policy makers. Often, individual corporations or businesses with similar goals form broad-based associations to further their general objectives. These umbrella organizations include the California Manufacturers and Technology Association, the California Business Alliance (for small enterprises), the California Bankers Association, and the California Council for Environmental and Economic Balance (for utilities and oil companies). The California Chamber of Commerce alone boasts 14,000 member companies with one-fourth of the state's private sector workforce. Each year, the Chamber publishes a list of "job killer" bills under consideration and then produces a report on the final outcome, which shows defeat of most of the list by either the legislature or a governor's veto. In 2015, the Chamber was successful in defeating eighteen out of nineteen bills it opposed as harmful to business.

Agribusiness is particularly active, because farming depends on government management of issues such as water availability and pesticide regulation. Large farming operations maintain their own lobbyists, but various producer groups also form associations. Most of the state's winemakers, for example, are represented by the 1,000-member Wine Institute. The California Cotton Ginners Association has only twenty-three members, yet produces between 2.0 and 2.5 million bales of cotton annually worth more than $1 billion. Broader organizations, such as the California Farm Bureau Federation, one of the state's most powerful lobby groups, speak for agribusiness in general by representing 78,000 members with crops equaling $56 billion in value.

Recently, high-tech industries have asserted their interests on a range of issues. Organizations such as TechNet, the Silicon Valley Leadership Group, and the American Electronics Association have lobbied for regulatory changes, tax relief, research and development tax credits, better education, "green" incentives in new areas such as solar energy, and other changes. The tech-heavy Silicon Valley Leadership Group alone represents 400 companies that provide $3 trillion worth of services and products in the global economy, an amount larger than the entire gross domestic product of the United Kingdom.

Professional Associations and Unions

Professional associations such as the California Medical Association (CMA), the California Association of Realtors (CAR), and the CAC are among the state's most active groups, and they are regularly among the largest campaign contributors. Other professionals, such as chiropractors, optometrists, dentists, accountants, engineers, and general contractors, also maintain active associations. Because many of these professionals serve the public, they often promote their concerns as broader than self-interest. Their credibility is further enhanced by the expertise they possess in their respective fields.

Teachers' associations and other public employee organizations fall somewhere between business associations and labor unions. Their members view themselves as professionals but in recent years have increasingly resorted to traditional labor union tactics, among them collective bargaining, strikes, and political campaign donations. Other public workers, including the highway patrol, corrections officers, and state university professors, have their own organizations.

Unions have done well in California, which ranks sixth among the fifty states in per capita union membership. Unions here represent 15.9 percent of the workforce, compared with 11.1 percent nationwide. Traditional labor unions represent nurses, machinists, carpenters, public utility employees, and dozens of other occupations. In the past few years, they have persuaded the legislature to enact the nation's first paid family leave program, allowing workers to take leave from their jobs for up to six weeks, and provide paid paternity leave, which also was the first program of its kind in the nation. In 2016, unions were instrumental in persuading the governor and legislature to increase the state's minimum wage to $15 per hour by 2021, well beyond the federal minimum wage of $7.25.

Perhaps the most controversial union in state politics is the California Correctional Peace Officers Association (CCPOA), which contributed $600,000 to the reelection campaign of Governor **Gray Davis** in 2002, just before the governor signed a three-year pay increase of 35 percent in the midst of a huge state budget deficit. The agreement fueled the accusation that Davis was a tool of major contributors, and became part of the argument to remove Davis from office. Davis was recalled in 2003 and replaced by Arnold Schwarzenegger. Undaunted, the 30,000-member CCPOA has persevered. Between 2003 and 2012, CCPOA collected more than $13 million from its members for campaign contributions. In the first few months of 2016 alone, CCPOA amassed a war chest exceeding $16 million, with much of the money dedicated to fighting state ballot issues on early prisoner release (Proposition 57) and ending capital punishment (Proposition 62). The CCPOA still wins some battles, but not as many as in the past.[1]

Demographic Groups

Groups that depend more on large membership numbers than on money can be described as **demographic groups**. Based on characteristics that distinguish their members from other segments of the population, such as their ethnicity, gender, or age, such groups usually focus on overcoming discrimination. Most major racial and ethnic organizations fall into this category.

One of the earliest demographic groups in California was the Colored Convention, which fought for the rights of African Americans in California in the nineteenth century. Today, several such groups advocate for African Americans, Asian Americans, and Native Americans. The United Farm Workers (UFW), GI Forum, Mexican American Legal Defense Fund (MALDEF), and Mexican American Political Association (MAPA) represent Latinos and immigrant issues.

The National Organization for Women (NOW), EMILY's List (EMILY is short for "early money is like yeast"), and National Women's Political Caucus (NWPC) actively support female candidates and feminist causes. Unlike some of the other statewide organizations, most of these groups are better organized at the local level than at the state level.

Several organizations have become prominent over the question of sexual equality. Gender equality groups (Gay, Lesbian, Bisexual, Transgender, also known as LGBT) have increased in numbers and voice in recent years, particularly over the issue of same-sex marriage. Equality California, the largest, has worked to elect LGBT legislators, obtain passage of equal rights legislation, and pursue same-sex marriage through both the courts and the legislative process. They have been opposed by groups like Campaign for California Families, which define marriage as a union only between a man and a woman.

With California's rapidly growing aging population heavily dependent on public services, this demographic also plays a pronounced role in state politics. Organizations such as AARP (formerly the American Association of Retired Persons), with 3 million members in California, have achieved a high profile in state politics, particularly on health care issues.

Single-Issue Groups

The groups discussed so far tend to have broad bases and deal with a wide range of issues. Another type of interest group operates with an extensive base of support for the resolution of narrow issues. **Single-issue groups** push for a specific question to be decided on specific terms. They support only candidates who agree with their particular position on an issue. The California Abortion Rights Action League (CARAL), for example, endorses only candidates who support a woman's right to choose (pro-choice), whereas antiabortion (or pro-life) groups such as the ProLife Council work only for candidates on the opposite side. Likewise, the Howard Jarvis Taxpayers Association evaluates candidates and ballot propositions solely in terms of whether they meet the association's objective of no unnecessary taxes and no wasteful government spending. Antitax groups have been very effective, especially with Republican legislators.

A single-interest group's potential ability to garner massive numbers of voters on a controversial issue can affect the outcome of an election and thus enhance its clout, at least on a temporary basis. That's what happened in 1994 when then–Republican Governor **Pete Wilson** sailed to reelection on the tailwind of "Save Our State," an anti-immigrant proposition supported by the California Coalition for Immigration Reform. But times change, and so do compositions of the electorate. In 2016, the voters swept away the last vestige of Wilson's anti-immigration platform when they passed Proposition 58, which restored bilingual education.

Public Interest Groups

Although virtually all organized interest groups claim to speak for the broader public interest, some groups clearly do not seek private gain and thus more correctly can claim to be **public interest groups**. These groups are distinguished from other organizations by the fact that they pursue goals to benefit society, not just their members.

Some public interest groups, such as California OneCare, have been instrumental in the fight for health care reform. In 2016, several health groups including the CMA and California Health Association teamed up with several children's advocate groups to take on big tobacco in an effort (**Proposition 56**) to raise per-pack taxes by $2.00.[2] Twice before in recent years, tobacco companies badly outspent proponents to defeat proposed increases, but not this time. Proposition 56 prevailed.

Often, public interest groups assume defensive postures to prevent abuse by companies or groups that threaten the public good. That's what happened in 2010, when TURN led a coalition of consumer groups against a Pacific Gas and Electric company (PG&E)–sponsored ballot proposition that would have made it very difficult for municipalities to purchase renewable power. The consumer groups triumphed, even though they were badly outspent by the utility and its allies by a margin of 19,565 to 1.

Environmental organizations such as the Sierra Club and Friends of the Earth have been very active in California with regard to water management, fracking, offshore oil drilling, air pollution, transportation, and pesticide use. Another important concern of these groups is land use, both for private development in sensitive areas and for public lands, which make up half the state. Surveys have reported that one in nine Californians claims membership in an environmental group.[3] The Sierra Club alone has more than 150,000 members in California.

Other public interest groups, such as the California Public Interest Research Group (CALPIRG), the California Budget Project, Common Cause, and the League of Women Voters, focus on governmental reform, campaign finance, voter participation, and civic engagement.

A final type of public interest group isn't really a group at all: local governments. Cities, school districts, special districts, and counties all lobby the state government for funding through organizations such as the League of California Cities, the California School Boards Association (CSBA), and the California State Association of Counties (CSAC). Dozens of cities and counties employ their own lobbyists in Sacramento, as do other governmental agencies. One study found that local governments collectively spend more on lobbying than organized labor, oil companies, or businesses.[4] As with traditional interest groups, they also endorse ballot measures that affect their interests and, on rare occasions, even sponsor initiatives.

Unlike other groups, cities and counties cannot make campaign contributions, but they can speak out. In 2010, local governments banded together to promote **Proposition 22, the Local Taxpayers, Public Safety, and Transportation Act**, an initiative to keep the state government from borrowing or raiding funds that voters have dedicated to public safety.

TECHNIQUES AND TARGETS: INTEREST GROUPS AT WORK

Interest groups seek to influence public policy by persuading policy makers. The legislature, executive branch, courts, bureaucracy, and sometimes the people are thus the targets of the various techniques these groups may use. Their primary weapons include lobbying, campaign support, litigation, and direct democracy.

Lobbying

The term **lobbying** refers to the activity that once occurred in the foyers adjacent to the legislative chambers. Advocates for various causes or issues would buttonhole legislators on their way in or out of the chambers and make their cases. This still goes on in the offices and hallways of the capitol, as well as in nearby bars and restaurants and wherever else policy makers congregate. Lobbyists are so integral to the legislative process that they are commonly referred to as members of the "third house," alongside the assembly and senate.

Until the 1950s, lobbying was a crude and completely unregulated activity. Lobbyists lavished food, drink, gifts, and money on legislators in exchange for favorable votes. Today's lobbyists, however, are experts on the legislative process. Many have served as legislators or staff for legislators. Often, they focus on targeted legislative committees and leaders, lobbying the full legislature only as a last resort. Unlike old-time lobbyists, today's advocates must be well informed about their causes.

When inexperienced legislators are unable to grasp major issues, lobbyists fill the void, often by actually writing bill proposals for legislators. During the 2011–2012 legislative session, for example, 27 percent of the bills introduced by legislators were submitted on behalf of lobbyists.[5] Campaign contributions remain a major weapon for interest groups, although legislators and lobbyists alike assert that contributions buy access, not votes. Still, one strategist states that "the system favors the moneyed—and there's been no sign of political reform."[6] All of this makes lobbying not only a highly specialized profession but also an expensive activity. As an example, during the 2015 session, lobby firms spent about $312.7 million just to influence the legislature alone—up from $280 million in 2013. That averages $2.6 million per legislator.[7]

In addition to the legislature, knowledgeable professionals target the executive branch, from the governor down to the bureaucracy. The governor not only proposes the budget but also must respond to thousands of bills that await his or her approval or rejection. In the process, the governor frequently meets with lobbyists in an effort to find common ground on proposed legislation.[8]

Bureaucrats (see Chapter 7) also are targets of astute interest groups. The bureaucracy must interpret new laws and make future recommendations to the governor and legislature. Moreover, on questions ranging from tax exemptions to coastal access to energy regulations, bureaucrats often have the final say on how laws will work. One study on the implementation of AB 32, the Global Warming Solutions Act of 2006, found energy interests lobbying the California Air Resources Board more than the governor or legislature to gain favorable regulations. In the words of one lobbyist, "I'm not going to say we love the thing [AB 32], but if that's the way the state wants to go … we want to make sure that we write regulations that we can comply with and are feasible to do."[9] Sometimes lobbyists will offer "talking points" to help bureaucrats justify their decisions on public matters. "It's called 'spoon feeding,'" a lobbyist recently explained to a California coastal commissioner regarding a matter before the commission, "but we're happy to do it."[10]

Lately, the public has become a target of lobbying, too. In media-addicted California, groups have begun making their cases through newspaper and television advertising between elections. Health care, education, energy, Indian gaming, and other issues have been subjects of costly media campaigns with the intent to motivate voters to communicate with state leaders.

Professional Lobbyists.   Between 1977 and 2015, the number of registered lobbyists in Sacramento more than doubled, from 582 to about 1,200, including about fifty former legislators. That's about ten lobbyists per legislator. State law prevents former legislators from lobbying for one year after they leave office, but as one legislator has noted, "I would certainly be available to give people political advice."[11] Even at that, legislators often wait out the transition year by serving as "consultants"—one more example of the blurry connection between those in and out of elected office.

Most lobbyists represent a particular business, union, organization, or group. Others are **contract lobbyists**, advocates who work for several clients simultaneously. Whether contract or specialized, more and more lobbyists make a career of their professions, accruing vast knowledge and experience. These professionals became even more influential when term limits eliminated senior legislators with countervailing knowledge, although some lobbyists complain that they must constantly reestablish their credibility with new decision makers. One prominent lobbyist, however, explained his lack of concern about term limits or other reforms: "Whatever your rules are, I'm going to win."[12]

Nonprofessional Lobbyists.   Some groups can't afford to hire a lobbyist, so they rely on their members instead. Even groups with professional help occasionally use their members to show elected officials the breadth of their support. Typically, this sort of lobbying is conducted by individuals who live in the districts of targeted legislators.[13] In addition, groups sometimes gather in mass at the capitol for demonstrations or concurrent lobbying of many elected officials.

Grassroots efforts by **nonprofessional lobbyists** have special credibility with legislators, but well-financed groups have learned to mimic grassroots efforts by forming front groups with grand names that conceal their real interests. In 2014, for example, legislators considered a bill requiring adult film workers to wear condoms during sexual acts in the name of health safety. After three efforts in the assembly, legislators passed the bill and sent it to the senate. The primary opposition came from a group known as the Free Speech Coalition (FSC), a porn industry–funded group purportedly concerned with government efforts to limit free speech. In this case, the FSC representatives argued that the condom law was intended to "exploit performers for political gain." The bill died in the Senate Appropriations Committee. By claiming concern for free expression, the porn industry appeared less self-serving and provided the logic for legislators to defeat the bill. Yet their victory was ratified in 2016, when the voters defeated **Proposition 60**, an initiative that would have required adult actors to carry out much of the objectives in the original bill.

Campaign Support

Most groups also try to further their cause by helping sympathetic candidates win election and reelection, commonly through financial contributions to their campaigns. Groups with limited financial resources contribute by providing volunteers to go door to door or to serve as phone-bank callers for candidates. Recently, they also have turned to social media outlets such as Facebook and Twitter to extend their influence and even promote voter turnout. Labor unions typically fall into this category, along with public education and environmental interests. Business groups, however, tend to be the most successful in having their way through generous financial support.

Take the issue of automobile passenger transportation companies. In recent years, Uber and Lyft have introduced a new approach for people to ferry passengers in their own automobiles, rather than a taxi. With their traditional business model threatened, taxi companies demanded that drivers of the new ride-hailing companies go through the same screening process as taxi drivers. Uber and Lyft resisted in a way familiar to Sacramento politics. During the 2015–2016 legislative session, the two companies contributed more than $900,000 to state legislators. Suddenly, three different bills were introduced to pave the way for the new transportation model. Meanwhile, the legislature spurned a bill that would have tightened background checks similar to those required of taxi drivers.[14] Table 4.1 shows the largest campaign contributor groups for 2014.

Campaign contributors claim that their money merely buys them access to decision makers. The press and the public often suspect a more conspiratorial

T A B L E 4.1 Top Ten Campaign Contributor Groups, 2014

Category	Money ($)
Party Committees	28,525,171
General Trade Unions	19,340,099
Public Sector Unions	14,158,838
Lawyers and Lobbyists	9,691,928
Real Estate	9,278,110
Insurance	6,995,967
Health Professionals	6,721,984
Tribal Governments	5,716,959
Telecom Services	4,382,909
Pharmaceuticals and Health Products	4,102,011

SOURCE: Institute on Money in State Politics, www.followthemoney.org.

arrangement, however, and evidence of money-for-votes trades has emerged in recent years. In 1994, fourteen people, including five state legislators, were convicted of exchanging favors for campaign contributions. The sting operation, known as "Shrimpscam" for an imaginary shrimp-catching company seeking tax benefits, shook Sacramento to its core. More recently, individual legislators have found themselves in trouble, usually for accepting contributions in exchange for promised legislative action. In 2014, State Senator Leland Yee was indicted for trading favors in Sacramento for bribes; he pled guilty in 2016 and was sentenced to five years in prison. In the same year, State Senator Ron Calderon was indicted for soliciting and accepting $100,000 in bribes from a health care company; he pled guilty in 2016 and was sentenced to three and one half years in prison.

These scandals show the potential for corruption to occur in California. As a result of the prosecution of such behaviors, politicians and contributors probably exercise greater caution. Still, the high cost of campaigning means that candidates continue to ask and lobbyists and interest groups continue to give. However, it is significant that the campaign funds come from a variety of interest groups, as well as other sources, making it difficult for any single group to prevail.

Litigation

Litigation is an option when a group questions the legality of legislation. In recent years, many groups have turned to the courts to challenge state laws, regulations, and actions by the executive branch in court. In 2014, a group of students sued state teachers associations on the grounds that the state laws for teacher tenure and other job protections denied students the best possible education. Initially, a superior court judge found for the plaintiffs, but in 2016, a state appeals court overturned the lower court ruling.

Over the years, interested organizations have also raised legal challenges to several successful ballot measures—including measures on immigration, affirmative action, campaign finance, bilingual education, and same-sex marriage—hoping that the initiatives would be declared unconstitutional. One such petition emerged in 2011 after the state adopted a voter-approved initiative that established the California Citizens Redistricting Commission. Members of the state Republican Party contended that redistricting was the responsibility of the legislature, which was the case until passage of the initiative. The state supreme court sided with the voters.

Direct Democracy

In his 1911 inaugural address, Governor **Hiram Johnson** championed direct democracy as the ultimate custodian of the legislative process. A century later, however, only broad-based or well-financed groups have the resources to collect the necessary signatures or to pay for expensive campaigns. **Direct democracy** gives interest groups the opportunity to promote their policy proposals through initiatives and referenda.

Sometimes, interest groups mobilize to gain passage of a ballot proposition; at other times, they work to defeat one. In 1998, for example, tribal supporters of gambling on Indian lands spent $10 million qualifying an initiative for the ballot in just thirty days—the most expensive petition drive in history. The voters ultimately approved the initiative. In 2008, the voters were asked to ratify four new agreements allowing Indian casinos to add 17,000 slot machines to the 62,000 already in place, providing the state with $450 million in new revenues. The pro-gaming interests spent more than $150 million on campaign activities—far exceeding the "no" side, which spent less than $40 million. The ballot propositions sailed through.

Sometimes big money is used to defeat a ballot proposition. In 2016, a group of reformers qualified an initiative, **Proposition 61**, which, if passed, would have required state agencies to pay the lowest prices for prescription drugs secured by the U.S. Department of Veterans Affairs. If passed, the new rules would have threatened the profit margins of major pharmaceutical companies. By the end of the fall campaign, opponents raised more than $110 million, most of which was used to blanket the airwaves with claims of the harm that would come to prescription buyers should the measure pass. The proposition was defeated.

The recall is also sometimes used by interest groups, usually to remove local elected officials. Teachers' unions, conservative Christians, and minority groups have conducted recall campaigns against school trustees, for example. These efforts, however, pale in comparison with the successful 2003 recall effort against Governor Gray Davis. The People's Advocate, a conservative antitax group, was among the leading forces early in that recall effort. During the campaign, groups ranging from the Howard Jarvis Taxpayers Association to the League of Conservation Voters weighed in on the issue.

REGULATING GROUPS

Free spending by interest groups and allegations of corruption led to the Political Reform Act of 1974 (introduced in Chapter 3), an initiative sponsored by Common Cause. Overwhelmingly approved by the voters, the law requires politicians to report their assets, disclose contributions, and declare how they spend campaign funds. Other provisions compel lobbyists to register with the secretary of state, file quarterly reports on their campaign-related activities, and reveal the beneficiaries of their donations. The measure also established the **Fair Political Practices Commission (FPPC)**, an independent regulatory body, to monitor these activities. When the commission finds incomplete or inaccurate reporting, it may fine the violator. Of greater concern than the financial penalty, however, is the bad press for those who incur the commission's reprimand.

The voters approved tightened rules in 1996, when they enacted strict limits on interest groups' practice of rewarding supportive legislators with travel and generous fees for speeches. In 2000, voters approved yet another initiative, which placed new constraints on political action committees and attempted to limit contributions to political campaigns. Yet between self-financed campaigns and the vigorous activities of groups engaged in independent expenditures, any thoughts of reduced spending quickly vanished.

MEASURING GROUP CLOUT: MONEY, NUMBERS, AND CREDIBILITY

Campaign regulations are generally intended to reduce the disproportionate influence of moneyed interests in state politics, but economic groups still have the advantage. Their stable of resources gives them the staying power to outlast the enthusiasm and energy of grassroots groups.

Public interest groups and demographic groups, however, gain strength from numbers, credibility, and motives other than self-interest. Occasionally they prevail, such as in 2010, when financially impotent public interest groups won the battle against utility company PG&E, which had qualified an initiative that would have made it nearly impossible for municipalities to purchase renewable energy. More commonly, economic interest groups affected by potentially harmful new costs rise to the occasion, whether the issue is health care, tobacco, oil, environmental protection, or other proposals that can increase the costs of doing business.

How powerful are interest groups and their lobbyists? It's hard to tell, but a 2010 survey found that 60 percent of lobbyist-sponsored bills become law, as compared with 40 percent of those not sponsored by lobbyists. First-time legislators were the most influenced, with the majority of their bills sponsored by lobbyists. At a minimum, interest groups have powerful connections with legislators.[15]

Whatever the balance among groups, they are central to California politics. In a political environment characterized by weak political parties and direct democracy, California's myriad interests have plenty of opportunity to thrive.

NOTES

1. "CCPOA's Clout High, but Profile Low," *Capitol Weekly* (Sacramento, CA), November 19, 2014.
2. "Billionaire-Back Campaign Launched to Raise California's Tobacco Tax," *Los Angeles Times*, May 17, 2016, www.latimes.com/politics/la-pol-sac-tobacco-tax -20160517-snap-story.html.
3. Public Policy Institute of California, *Statewide Survey*, June 2000, www.ppic.org.
4. "Cities, Counties, Pay Price for Capitol Clout," *Los Angeles Times*, September 10, 2007, pp. B1, B4.
5. "California Legislation Often 'Sponsored'—or Even Written—by Interest Groups," *Sacramento Bee*, April 28, 2013, www.sacbee.com/2013/04/28/5377329 /california-legislation-often-sponsored.html.
6. "Special Interests: How They Get around Voter-Approved Limits on Campaign Contributions," *San Francisco Chronicle*, February 11, 2008, pp. A1, A6.
7. "California Lobbying Tops $300 Million in 2015," *Sacramento Bee*, February 2, 2016, www.sacbee.com/news/politics-government/capitol-alert/article57960523 .html.
8. See "A Lobbyist by Any Other Name?" *San Jose Mercury News*, May 20, 2005, pp. 1A, 17A.
9. "Lobbyists Heat Up over Climate Law," *Sacramento Bee*, July 12, 2010, pp. A1, A10.
10. "E-Mails Put California Coastal Commissioner in an Awkward Spot," *Los Angeles Times*, July 10, 2010, p. AA3.
11. "Elective Office Improves a Resume," *Los Angeles Times*, November 24, 2006, pp. B1, B11.
12. Douglas Foster, "The Lame Duck State," *Harper's*, February 1994.
13. "Business Interests Have an Edge in Lobbying," *San Francisco Chronicle*, December 26, 2011, pp. A1, A11.
14. "Uber, Lyft Learn How to Navigate Sacramento," *San Francisco Chronicle*, June 6, 2016, pp. A1, A7.
15. "Why Lobbyists Rule the Capitol," *San Jose Mercury News*, July 19, 2010, pp. 1, 6.

LEARN MORE ON THE WEB

California Association of Realtors (CAR):
www.car.org

California Chamber of Commerce:
www.calchamber.com

California Labor Federation:
www.calaborfed.org

California Technology Council:
www.californiatechnology.org

Common Cause:
  www.commoncause.org

Howard Jarvis Taxpayers Association:
  www.hjta.org

Latino Issues Forum:
  www.lif.org

League of Women Voters of California:
  www.ca.lwv.org

Sierra Club:
  www.sierraclub.org/ca

GET INVOLVED

Study which interest groups contribute to the campaigns of your local legislator over a recent legislative session, and explore whether any of those organizations sought legislation. Or you could volunteer or intern with a local group to learn more about their members, tactics, and issues.

5

The Legislature: The Perils of Policy Making

LEARNING OBJECTIVES

5.1 Compare the making and unmaking of a model legislature.

5.2 Clarify the leaders and their responsibilities.

5.3 Explain staffing the professional legislature.

5.4 Describe how a bill becomes a law.

5.5 Summarize the legislature's unfinished business.

Thousands of bills are passed in the California legislature every year. Some are narrow in focus, such as a law allowing adults to drink beer at farmers' markets (passed in 2015). Others are sweeping in impact, such as the law permitting physicians to prescribe lethal drug doses to terminally ill patients who want to end their lives (passed in 2015). A large portion of these laws may seem trivial to the casual observer, but the legislature is responsible for tackling the state's problems, big and small.

Of course, the legislature does not act in a policy-making vacuum; rather, it must share policy making with the other branches of government, particularly the executive branch, where the governor has final say over the bills that reach his desk. In addition, the legislature has internal problems to manage stemming from political and philosophical differences. These routinely occur not only internally among Democrats and Republicans, but also within and between the legislature's two chambers. As one beleaguered assembly member once said, "More times than not, it seems that we have four political parties in the legislature alone!" Partisanship and ideological schisms fracture the legislative process in California, and these stark divisions often leave the governing body tied in political knots.

Then there's the question of public policy priorities. Some observers have wondered in recent years how the legislature could immerse itself in issues such as regulations on imported kangaroo leather and shark fins, yet seemingly avoid substantive questions about tax reform, water policy, underfunded public education, and a frayed infrastructure. It's no wonder that a 2016 public opinion survey found the voters divided on the legislature's behavior, with 43 percent expressing approval and 37 percent declaring disapproval of the legislative branch of California's government. While the voters were hardly gushing with praise, their sentiments were much more positive than eight years earlier, when only 14 percent approved of the legislature's work.[1] Still, the legislature is the state institution that most directly links the people with their government. The question is, does it still do its job in the twenty-first century?

THE MAKING AND UNMAKING
OF A MODEL LEGISLATURE

Structurally and numerically, much of today's state legislature parallels its original design and intent. But changing circumstances in the state's political environment present a state legislative branch with characteristics considerably different than its national counterpart.

California's first constitution, in 1849, provided a **bicameral (two-house) legislature** similar to the U.S. Congress. Thirty years later, a revised state constitution fixed the senate at forty members serving four-year terms (with half the body elected every two years); the assembly was set at eighty members serving two-year terms. Those numbers and terms of office continue to this day. Throughout the first century of governance, legislators met on a part-time basis, with budgets crafted in two-year increments.

Beginning in 1926, assembly members were elected on the basis of population, like their counterparts in the U.S. House of Representatives; senators were elected by county in the same way that each state elects two U.S. senators.[2] The large number of lightly populated counties north of the Tehachapi Mountains enabled the rural north to dominate the state senate despite southern California's growth. By 1965, twenty-one of the forty state senators in California represented only 10 percent of the population; Los Angeles County, then home to 35 percent of the state's residents, had but a single state senator.

Then came change. The U.S. Supreme Court's *Reynolds v. Sims* decision in 1964 ordered all states to organize their upper chambers by population rather than by territory. The shift in representation led to more senators in southern California and the state's urban areas, with declines in rural and northern regions. The new legislators were younger, better educated, and more ideological; they also had more varied ethnic and gender backgrounds. In 1966, the voters created a full-time legislature with full-time salaries.

These days, the legislature meets an average of more than 200 days per year, with full-time salaries to match. As of 2017, the legislators' base salary is $104,115, the highest among the fifty states. Perks such as daily housing allowances when the legislature is in session push annual incomes close to $130,000.[3] Only nine other states have full-time legislatures.[4]

Term Limits

Once the legislature became a full-time body, some legislators were elected to several consecutive terms, similar to many members of Congress. For these individuals, experience became an important element of stewardship. But whereas elected officials viewed extensive experience as an asset, others viewed it as an impediment to governance and protection of the status quo. Over time, critics called for limits on legislative service. They believed that a "turnstile" type of legislature with restricted lengths of service would guarantee new faces, reduce the influence of money, and prevent incumbents from becoming entrenched in excess. In 1990 the voters passed **Proposition 140**, an initiative that limited elected executive branch officers and state senators to two 4-year terms and assembly members to three 2-year terms, while reducing the legislature's operating budget (and thus its staff) by 38 percent. Of the fifteen states currently with term limits, California has one of the most severe conditions in the nation. Unlike most other states with term limits, once state legislators in California complete their terms of service, they may never run for the legislature again.

Some objectives associated with **term limits** have been met, while others show no sign of coming to pass. New faces have certainly appeared—particularly women and minorities in much larger numbers than in the past—but in many cases legislators have simply jumped from one chamber to the other. Nevertheless, those from relatively affluent backgrounds continue to be elected to the legislature in disproportionate numbers. In this sense, little has changed.

There also have been increasing instances of political cannibalism. Some **termed-out** legislators in one branch have challenged members from their own political party who are eligible to serve another term in another branch. One such example occurred in 2016, when termed-out Democratic Speaker of the Assembly Tony Atkins of San Diego basically forced out incumbent Democratic Senator Marty Block, largely due to her superior fundraising capabilities. In other cases, termed-out legislators have returned home to run for county supervisor and other local government positions where they may continue service. State Senator Joe Simitian of Santa Clara County, formerly a county supervisor before his legislative years, won election again in 2012 as he neared completion of his last term in the Senate. Term limits may have limited the time of elected officials in the state legislature, but they have also spawned the state's version of "musical chairs" and contributed to higher campaign costs.

Research reveals a considerable decline in the quality of legislation since the adoption of term limits.[5] Some of this no doubt relates to the inability to acquire legislative knowledge because of rapid turnover. Inasmuch as legislators have little opportunity to gain expertise, they tend to rely more on the governor and lobbyists,[6] the former because of policy experts who work as aids in the governor's office, and the latter because of the permanence of the lobbyists in the state capital. Legislators may be termed out, but lobbyists are not. As a result of term limits, leadership positions in the legislature no longer carry the clout that once made that branch an effective counterweight to the executive branch. Clearly, problems can develop with erratic leadership changes and inexperienced leaders.

Some of these concerns may have been addressed with the passage of **Proposition 28** in 2012. Now, instead of tenure limitations in each chamber, legislators may serve in either chamber, but for no more than 12 years' total. Proponents of this proposition believe that the ability to stay in one chamber for a longer time will allow legislators to develop more expertise. Others aren't so sure, given that term limits still force legislators out of office, even those who perform superbly. Nevertheless, Assembly Member **Anthony Rendon**, elected to the speakership in 2015 after only three years in office, has the possibility of keeping his job for nearly a decade, assuming his party remains in the majority and he has no internal Democratic challenge.

Nationwide, the term-limits movement seems to be abating. Six states with term limits have rejected the concept since 1997—Idaho, Massachusetts, Mississippi, Oregon, Utah, and Washington. But in California, the voters continue to favor term limits. A public opinion poll in 2012 found that a resounding 62 percent of Californians supported the concept, compared with only 12 percent who rejected it.[7]

Redistricting

A related issue concerns the composition of districts. By law, every ten years after the national census, the state realigns congressional and state legislative districts to have approximately the same populations. This process is known as **redistricting**. Until 2011, redistricting was carried out by the legislature, as in most states. Legislators created districts that were numerically correct but with artificially high numbers of Democrats or Republicans fashioned to protect incumbents. Many districts were oddly shaped. For example, after the 2001 redistricting process, one senate district was 200 miles in length; others appeared almost as a Rorschach inkblot personality test. To many, the process seemed to be little more than an "incumbency protection plan."[8] As one legislator complained, "What happened to drawing lines for the people of the state rather than ourselves?"[9] During the entire decade between 2001 and 2010, only 1 of the 173 seats (120 in the state legislature and 53 in Congress) changed party hands.

On seven different occasions, the voters defeated ballot proposals to take redistricting away from the state legislators. But in 2008, the state's voters passed **Proposition 11, the Voters FIRST Initiative**, which gave redistricting responsibility to a new fourteen-member independent commission composed of five Democrats, five Republicans, and four members not affiliated with either major party. In 2011, after completion of the U.S. Census, the state's new **Citizens Redistricting Commission** realigned legislative districts to be equal in population once again—482,500 for each assembly district and 965,000 in each senate district. Unlike the legislature's previous efforts, however, the Commission considered community geography and neighborhood compositions over political advantages associated with incumbency. Figures 5.1 and 5.2 show the same area of southern California after the legislature's redistricting in 2001 and after the commission's work in 2011. Most districts now are much more compact than their predecessors. Voters FIRST sponsors hoped that passage would create a less partisan and more effective legislature, but few changes have been observed in the first few years of the new process. Table 5.1 displays the partisan breakdown of the legislature since 1985.

Redistricting, the change from part-time to full-time legislators, and term limits transformed the legislature, albeit unevenly. To be sure, the new framework attracted better educated and more professional individuals and also made election to office more feasible for women and minorities. Thus, after the 2016 elections, the assembly included 17 females, 22 Latinos, 9 African Americans, 10 Asian Americans, and 4 openly gay members; the senate included 9 females, 5 Latinos, 2 African Americans, 1 Asian American, and 4 openly gay members (see Figure 5.3).

Despite greater diversity, the legislature has narrowed in terms of vocational backgrounds. During the 1980s, legislative aspirants from the business world were flanked by large numbers of lawyers, local activists, educators, and former legislative aides. But increasingly, the "business candidate" has emerged as the dominant category of self-description. During the 1990s, about half of all legislative candidates on the ballot listed some form of business as their occupation. Beginning in the late 1990s, large numbers of people from city- and county-elected posts also took seats in the legislature. These patterns continue today.[10]

LEADERS

Although the two chambers share lawmaking responsibilities, they function differently. Because the assembly is larger, it is more hierarchical in organization. The **speaker of the assembly** is clearly in charge of that body and wields considerable power. The speaker controls the flow of legislation, designation of committee chairs and assignments, and distribution of vast campaign funds to the members of his or her political party. The number of standing, or topical, committees may vary with the speaker's term in office. For example, there were thirty-one such committees in the assembly during 2015–2016, one more than the previous session. Some legislative committees are far more important than others, so the speaker's friendship is of great value to a legislator.

By tradition, the party with a majority in the assembly chooses the speaker in a closed meeting, or caucus. A vote is then taken by the full assembly, with the choice already known to all. The minority party selects its leader in a similar fashion. Majority and minority floor leaders, as well as their whips (assistants), provide further support for the legislative officers. With solid majorities for

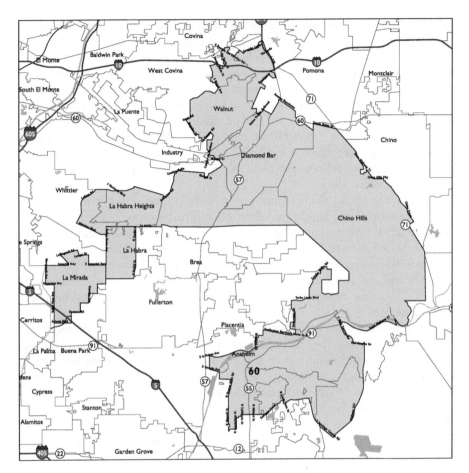

FIGURE 5.1 Map of Assembly District 60 after 2001 Redistricting.

most of the past half-century, the Democrats have controlled the speakership for all but four years during the period.

Before the term-limits era, speakers often held their posts for ten years or more. For the quarter century following Proposition 140, the tenures of speakers were limited to between one and four years. Anthony Rendon, the current speaker, may be the first to extend that tenure boundary, now that legislators may serve all of their time in one chamber for no more than 12 years.

Beyond tenure constraints, some speakers have reflected major changes in California values as well as politics. Toni Atkins, speaker between 2014 and 2016, was something of a trailblazer as the first lesbian to hold the post. Her predecessor, John Perez, was the first openly gay speaker.

In some respects, the senate has evolved even more than the assembly. Prior to the court-ordered redistricting in 1966, the senate emphasized collegiality and cooperation over strong leadership, strict rules, and partisan differences. But since then, the senate has become almost as partisan as the assembly. The most

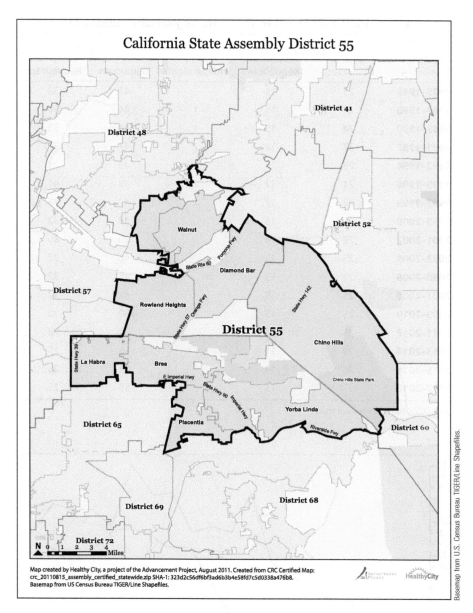

FIGURE 5.2 Map of Assembly District 55 after 2011 Redistricting.

powerful member is the **president pro tem**, who, like the speaker, is elected by the majority party after each general election. The minority party also elects its leader at that time. The key to senate power lies with the five-member **Rules Committee**, which is chaired by the president pro tem and controls all other committee assignments and the flow of legislation. In 2015–2016, the senate had twenty-two standing committees, the same number as the previous session.

TABLE 5.1 Political Parties in the State Legislature, 1985–2016

Legislative Session	Senate			Assembly	
	Democrats	Republicans	Independents	Democrats	Republicans
1985–1986	25	15		47	33
1987–1988	24	15	1	44	36
1989–1990	24	15	1	47	33
1991–1992	27	12	2	47	33
1993–1994	23	15	2	49	31
1995–1996	21	17	2	39	41
1997–1998	22	17	1	42	38
1999–2000	25	15		48	32
2001–2002	26	14		50	30
2003–2004	25	15		48	32
2005–2006	25	15		48	32
2007–2008	25	15		48	32
2009–2010	25	15		50	30
2011–2012	25	13		52	28
2013–2014	29	11		55	25
2015–2016	26	14		52	28
2017–2018	27	13		55	25

SOURCE: California Secretary of State.

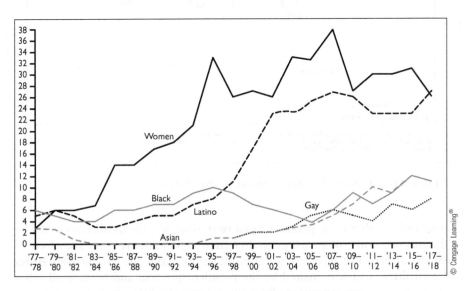

FIGURE 5.3 Women and Minorities in the California Legislature.

The current president pro tem, Democrat **Kevin de Leon**, was elected to the position in 2014. He will not be termed out until 2018. Like most others in leadership positions, de Leon assumed his post with relatively little senate experience, but his previous four years in the state assembly have enabled him to work well with the lower chamber. De Leon hasn't been shy about exercising his power. In 2015, Lieutenant Governor Gavin Newsom announced sponsorship of a strong statewide gun control initiative, despite de Leon's plea to leave the issue in the legislature's hands. When Newsom refused to defer, de Leon persuaded fellow Democrats to slash Newsom's office budget by one-third.[11]

Along with his power, de Leon's elevation has a symbolic value. His presence, along with Speaker Rendon, marks the first time that two Latino legislators have held the state's top legislative positions.

For the past few years, Democrats have enjoyed sizable majorities in the legislature. Between 2012 and 2014, Democrats even eclipsed the absolute two-thirds threshold necessary for urgency legislation, veto overrides, and tax increases. Some observers worried that the combination of a two-thirds majority might in both chambers and a Democratic governor might lead Democrats to raise taxes in support of an aggressive liberal agenda focusing on social welfare policies, but legislative leaders and the governor kept them in check.

The Democrats briefly lost their two-thirds senate majority in 2014. Some observers blamed the loss on then-President Pro Tem **Darrell Steinberg** for allowing ethical lapses, which led to suspensions of three senators. Others pointed to weakened leadership because of term limits, where the short periods of control have kept leaders from exercising control over their members.[12] Nevertheless, the Democrats regained a two-thirds senate majority in 2016, while maintaining their two-thirds majority in the assembly.

Democratic majorities in both chambers have led to ambitious efforts in numerous policy areas. In 2015, Democrats secured passage of the End of Life Option Act, allowing physicians to prescribe lethal doses of drugs to patients suffering from terminal diseases. During the same year, legislators passed the Fair Pay Act, which closed loopholes that allowed employers to pay women less than men when they do the same work. And in 2016, the legislature passed the Fair Wage Act of 2016, which placed the state on a path to a minimum wage of $15 per hour by 2022. Still, while Democrats have been in the overwhelming majority, many are political moderates and, as such, have been able to temper their more liberal colleagues. Thus in 2015, moderates watered down a proposed family leave policy, an ambitious proposed petroleum reduction use bill, and a proposal that would have greatly expanded child care benefits. Ironically, many of the moderate Democrats who joined against these proposals received campaign contributions from business interests that had supported Republicans in previous years.[13] These examples underscore the reality that the political party leaderships may have the numbers, but not always the votes.

STAFFING THE PROFESSIONAL LEGISLATURE

The evolution of the legislature into a full-time body was accompanied by a major expansion of its support staff. These days, about 2,200 staff assistants (commonly called "staffers") work for the members and committees—a far cry from the 485 employed by the last part-time legislature in 1966. Those in the capital usually concentrate on pending legislation and research, whereas staffers in the legislators' home district offices spend much of their time on constituents' problems.

Legislators spend much of their time in committees, the heart of the legislative process. Most committees cover specialized policy areas such as education or natural resources. A few, such as the senate and assembly rules committees, deal with procedures and internal organization. Each committee employs staff consultants who are experts on the committee's subject area and who are politically astute individuals in general—important attributes because they serve at the pleasure of the committee chair. Besides the standing committees, staffers assist more than sixty select committees that address narrow issues and nine joint committees that coordinate two-house policy efforts.

Another staff group is even more political. Employed by the Democratic and Republican caucuses in the senate and assembly, these assistants are supposed to deal with possible legislation. However, their real activities usually center on advancing the interests of their political party and its elected members.

In addition to personal, committee, and leadership staffers, legislators have created neutral support agencies. With a staff of fifty-six, the **legislative analyst** (a position created in 1941) provides fiscal expertise, reviewing the annual budget and assessing programs that affect the state's coffers. The **legislative counsel** (created in 1913) employs about eighty attorneys to draft bills for legislators and determine their potential impact on existing legislation. The **state auditor** (created in 1955) assists the legislature by periodically reviewing and evaluating ongoing programs.

Historically, staffing has enhanced the legislature's professionalism. Yet some staffers, especially those who work for the legislative leaders, clearly spend more time on partisan politics than on legislation. Many have used their positions as apprenticeships to gain skills and contacts for their own campaign efforts or future employment as lobbyists. All this, critics point out, is funded by the taxpayers. Defenders of the system counter that this staffing arrangement helps compensate for weak party organizations and the information gaps associated with rapid legislative turnover.

HOW A BILL BECOMES A LAW

The legislature passes laws. It also proposes constitutional amendments, which are submitted for voter approval after they receive absolute two-thirds majority votes in both chambers—that is, twenty-seven votes in the senate and fifty-four in the assembly. The same absolute two-thirds majority votes are required for the legislature to offer bond measures—money borrowed for long-term, expensive state projects. Proposed constitutional amendments and bond measures must then obtain majority votes at the next election before becoming law.

Most of the legislature's energy, however, is spent on lawmaking. Absolute majorities—twenty-one votes in the senate and forty-one votes in the assembly —are required to pass the annual budget and basic laws intended to take effect the following January, but absolute two-thirds votes in both chambers are required for urgency measures (those that become law immediately upon the governor's signature) and overrides of the governor's veto. The process, however, is far from simple.

The Formal Process

The legislative process begins when the assembly member or senator sponsoring a bill gives the clerk of the chamber a copy, which is recorded and numbered (see Figure 5.4). The process is known as moving the bill "across the desk" (of the receiving clerk), signifying that the proposed measure is now officially under consideration. The bill then undergoes three readings in the chamber of the author (assembly or senate) and several committee hearings before it is sent to the other chamber, where the process is repeated. The first reading simply acknowledges the bill's submission.

Depending upon the chamber of origin, either the senate Rules Committee or the assembly Rules Committee decides on the route of the bill. The chairs of these important committees can affect a bill's fate by sending it to "friendly" or "hostile" committees and by assigning it a favorable or unfavorable route. Typically, a bill is assigned to two or three committees for careful scrutiny by members whose responsibilities include that bill's subject area. More than half of all bills die in committee, either through a formal vote or because the chair decides not to call for a vote.

Typically, between 4,000 and 5,000 bills are introduced during each two-year session, with assembly members limited to fifty proposals and senators limited to sixty-five. Given such volume, the **legislative committees** are essential to getting laws passed. They hold hearings, debate, and may eventually vote on each bill delegated to them. Most committees deal in narrow areas, but a few—such as the senate Budget and Fiscal Review Committee and the assembly Committee on Appropriations—focus on the collection and distribution of funds and thus enjoy clout that goes beyond any one policy area.

At the conclusion of its hearings, a committee can kill a bill, release it without recommendation, or approve it with a "do pass" proposal. It may also recommend approval contingent on certain changes or amendments, which can be substantial or minor and technical. Only when a bill receives a positive recommendation from all of the committees to which it was assigned is it likely to get a second reading by the full legislative body. At this stage, the chamber considers additional amendments. After all proposed revisions have been discussed, the bill is printed in its final form and presented to the full chamber membership for a third reading. After further debate on the entire bill, a vote is taken.

Sometimes, the bill changes so dramatically that the original author abandons sponsorship in disgust; the bill then dies unless another legislator assumes sponsorship. On other occasions, a bill is introduced about a topic of little significance

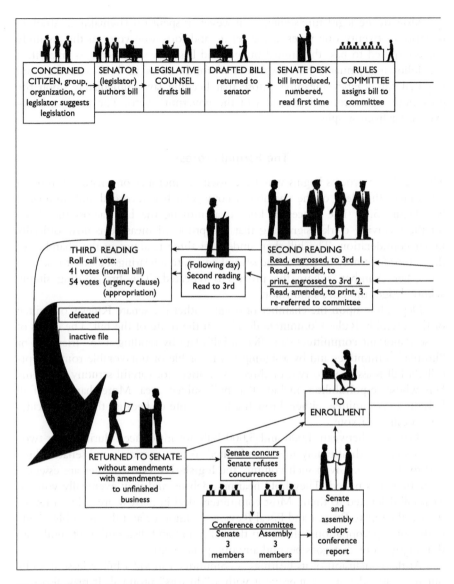

FIGURE 5.4 How a Bill Becomes a Law.

or with little more than a number. Then, later in the term, when the deadline for introductions has passed, the author may strip the bill of its original language and offer replacement language to deal with a pressing topic new to the legislative agenda. This strategy, known as **gut-and-amend**, isn't pretty but gives a legislator flexibility that he or she would not have otherwise. It also circumvents the normal legislative process of committee hearings and due deliberation, sometimes to the chagrin of lobbyists, interest groups, or a confused general public.

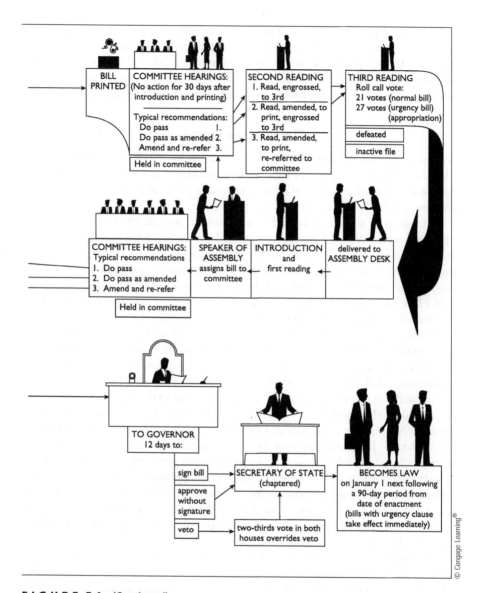

FIGURE 5.4   (Continued)

If a bill is approved by the members of one chamber, it goes to the other chamber, where the process starts anew. Again, the bill may die anywhere along the perilous legislative path. If the two chambers pass different versions of the same bill, the versions must be reconciled by a **conference committee**. Senate members are appointed by the Rules Committee; assembly members are chosen by the speaker, yet another sign of the power that comes with that position. If the conference committee agrees on a single version and if both chambers approve it by the required margins, the bill goes to the governor for his or her approval. Otherwise, the proposed legislation is dead.

Usually, a bill becomes law if the governor signs it or takes no action within twelve days. However, if it is passed immediately before a session's end, the governor has thirty days to act. If the governor vetoes a bill, an absolute two-thirds majority must be attained in both houses for it to become law. Attaining such a lopsided vote is next to impossible, so vetoed bills generally fall by the wayside.

The Informal Process

Politics permeates the formal, "textbook" process by which a bill becomes law. This means that every piece of legislation is considered not only on its merits but also on the basis of a variety of factors, including political support, interest group pressure, public opinion, and personal power.

Members of the majority party chair most, if not all, of the committees in any given year. With Democrats in control for most of the past five decades, they have reaped the benefits of the committee chairs (particularly extra staff and procedural advantages), secured the best committee assignments, and been assigned the most spacious offices. Likewise, when assembly Republicans briefly held a bare majority in 1996, they assumed control of twenty-five of the twenty-six committees at the time, and the benefits were reversed.

Political support within the legislature is essential to numerous decisions. So many bills flow through the process that members often vote on measures they haven't even read, relying on staff, committee, or leadership recommendations. Sometimes, a bill's fate rests with key legislative leaders, who can use their positions to stifle or speed up a proposal at various points in the legislative process. In the assembly, the speaker may actually appoint extra members to a committee temporarily to move a bill along. Outcomes are also affected by **logrolling**, a give-and-take bargaining process in which legislators agree to support each other's bills. More often than not, legislators give away their votes on matters of little concern to them in hopes of mollifying opponents or pleasing powerful leaders. And on occasion, some members of the assembly have been known to cast the votes of other members by clicking their electronic devices. This illegal activity, called **ghost voting**,[14] can't take place in the senate, where members cast votes by a show of hands.

In addition to the work of elected officials, public opinion also affects legislation, sometimes dramatically. Recent statutes on children's safety and health, cell-phone use while driving, higher education opportunities for illegal immigrants, environmental quality, and homeowners' rights have been enacted in direct response to public concern.

And, of course, we can't forget the influence of interest groups. As noted in Chapter 4, pressure from interest groups permeates the legislative process, with many bills actually written for legislators by lobbyists.

The relationship between the private and public policy arenas has only intensified with the growth of a full-time, year-round, term-limited legislature. The combined cost of legislative campaigns has soared from $7 million in 1966 to $107 million in 2014. With an average of just under $1 million per legislative seat, California's legislative elections are the most expensive state contests in the nation.[15] And, given the millions of dollars spent by independent expenditure committees that were not tied officially to any candidate, the total spent on legislative campaigns in the state in all likelihood exceeded $150 million. Much of this money, of course, comes from interest groups.

OTHER FACTORS

Personal power within the legislature remains a component of the political process, especially in cases of conflict. One such example occurred in 2008, when then–Senate President Pro Tem Don Perata and the Democratic majority of the senate Rules Committee blocked four Schwarzenegger nominees to the twelve-member California Parole Board. For months, Perata had complained about California's low parole rate, implying that the problem rested with the parole board. This action sent a clear message to both the board and the governor.[16]

Sometimes the mere threat of an initiative spurs legislative action. In 2016, proponents advocating a $15 minimum wage in California abandoned an initiative effort after the legislature and Governor Jerry Brown agreed to pass legislation on the issue. The bill did not give the would-be initiative supporters everything they sought, but it came close enough that supporters decided to refrain from a costly statewide election. Conversely, the legislature's law that banned plastic bags in 2014 was nearly undone in November 2016 by a business-sponsored referendum to cancel the law. On this occasion, the voters elected to let the environmentally friendly law remain in place.

UNFINISHED BUSINESS

Today's legislature faces myriad issues, ranging from a poorly working public education system to a deteriorating infrastructure. Faced with revolving participants and competing political objectives, the legislature operates with little stability and less tradition. Term limits, rollercoaster state budgets (see Chapter 8), and an uneven economy for most of the past decade have added to the challenges for policy making. All this is folded into what one recent study finds the most polarized political environment of the fifty state legislatures.[17]

With all these pressures, more often legislators often seem to react to problems rather than to anticipate or solve them. As a consequence, public policies are made increasingly by initiative, the governor, or the courts. Nevertheless, the legislature continues to grapple with the leading issues of the day, and at least sometimes, lawmakers manage to overcome assorted obstacles in a fractured political environment to enact policies of substance.

NOTES

1. "Californians and Their Government," Public Policy Institute of California, May 2016, p. 15.

2. In general, the plan provided one senator per county. In a few cases, two low-populated counties shared a senator, and in one case, three low-populated counties—Alpine, Inyo, and Mono—shared a senator.

3. Legislators receive monthly allowances for cars (including gasoline and mainte-nance); life, health, dental, vision, and disability insurance; and a daily housing allowance when they are in session in Sacramento. On average. these benefits amount to about $27,000 annually, almost all of which is nontaxable.

4. The other full-time legislatures are Alaska, Florida, Massachusetts, Michigan, New Jersey, New York, Ohio, Pennsylvania, and Wisconsin.

5. See Bruce E. Cain and Thad Kousser, "Adapting to Term Limits in California: Recent Experiences and New Directions," Joint Project on Term Limits, National Conference on State Legislatures, 2005.

6. "Report Chronicles Downside of Term Limits," Stateline.org, August 16, 2006, www.stateline.org/live/details/story?contentId=134247.

7. "Drop in Support for Cigarette Tax, Most Support Term Limits Change," Public Policy Institute of California (San Francisco: PPIC, May 23, 2012).

8. "Plan to Redraw Districts Passes," *Los Angeles Times,* September 14, 2001, p. B8.

9. *Ibid.*

10. See Bruce E. Cain and That Kousser, *op. cit.,* p. 15.

11. "A rising force, moderate Democrats put their stamp on California legislative session," *Sacramento Bee,* September 12, 2015, www.sacbee.com/news/politics -government/capitol-alert/article35072760.html (accessed July 9, 2016).

12. "State's power needle points south," *Los Angeles Times,* January 23, 2014, pp. AA1, AA8.

13. "Ethical Lapses Illustrate Limits of Leader's Power," *San Jose Mercury News,* March 31, 2014, pp. 1, 6.

14. See "Ghost Voting: A Long History," *San Francisco Chronicle,* June 10, 2008, pp. A1, A16.

15. Institute for State Government and Politics, http://maplight.org/california /contributions?s=1&office_party=Senate%2CAssembly%2CDemocrat%2CRepublican % 2CIndependent&election=2012&business_sector=any&business_industry =any&source=All

16. "Dems Reject Two of Schwarzenegger's Parole Appointees," *Sacramento Bee,* June 26, 2008, p. A3.

17. "How U.S. State Legislatures are Polarized and Getting More Polarized," *Washington Post,* January 14, 2014, www.washingtonpost.com/news/monkey-cage/wp /2014/01/14/how-u-s-state-legislatures-are-polarized-and-getting-more-polarized -in-2-graphs/ (accessed July 9, 2016).

LEARN MORE ON THE WEB

California State Assembly:
www.assembly.ca.gov

California State Senate:
www.senate.ca.gov

Campaign finance:
www.followthemoney.org

Daily politics and policy-related news:
    www.rtumble.com
    www.calmatters.com

Legislative Analyst's Office:
    www.lao.ca.gov

Legislative histories and bill analyses:
    www.leginfo.ca.gov/bilinfo.html

National Conference of State Legislatures:
    www.ncsl.org

Search for your legislator:
    www.legislature.ca.gov/legislators_and_districts/districts/districts.html

Watch or listen to the legislature in session:
    www.legislature.ca.gov/the_state_legislature/calendar_and_schedules
    /audio_tv.html

GET INVOLVED

Ask your local state legislator for a list of his or her pending bills, and track one of them as it goes through the legislative process. To find your representatives, go to: www.legislature.ca.gov/legislators_and_districts/districts/districts.html.

6

California Law: Politics and the Courts

LEARNING OBJECTIVES

6.1 Describe the structure of the California court system.

6.2 Understand how judges are selected in California.

6.3 Explain how courts are part of the political process.

6.4 Consider the role of the courts regarding the death penalty, same-sex marriage, and managing the prison population.

We know that courts are a fundamental element of government—one of the three essential branches—but are they "political"? Don't they just administer the law? Criminal defendants are found guilty or not guilty based on the evidence and sentenced accordingly, while parties to civil cases win or lose according to the facts of the case. But, of course, it's not always so simple. Prosecutors have discretion about the cases they bring forward and the charges they make; defendants or parties to civil cases have varying degrees of resources to make their cases; and, perhaps most significantly, judges also have discretion about the conduct of trials and the sentences they render.

But courts are also political because their judgments are choices between public policy alternatives. When judges consider cases, they evaluate the issues before them both in terms of existing law and in the context of the California and U.S. Constitutions. Rulings based on differing judicial interpretations of these documents help some people and hurt others. In California, court decisions overturning popular initiatives have made us particularly mindful of judicial politics. Beyond all this, courts are political because judges are appointed by politicians—governors and presidents—and, in California, judges periodically go before the voters.

All this explains why the courts, like members of the executive and legislative branches, are subject to the attentions and pressures of California's competing interests. This is why the courts are political.

THE CALIFORNIA COURT SYSTEM

The California court system is the largest in the nation, with over 2,000 judicial officers and 19,000 court employees. The system has three levels (see Figure 6.1) that are linked, but each has its own responsibilities. Most cases begin and end at the lowest level. Only a few move up the state's judicial ladder through the appeals process, and even fewer end up in the U.S. Supreme Court.

A Hierarchy of Courts

The vast majority of cases begins and ends in trial courts, the bottom rung of the judicial ladder. In California, **superior courts** in each county are the trial courts, handling misdemeanor cases (minor crimes, including most traffic offenses), felonies (serious crimes subject to sentences of a year or more in state prison), civil suits (noncriminal disputes), divorces, and juvenile cases. Superior courts also operate small claims courts, where individuals can take cases with damage claims up to $10,000 before a judge without attorneys—sort of like television's *Judge Judy*.

Losers in trial courts may ask the court on the next rung of the judicial ladder to review the decision. Most cases aren't appealed, but when major crimes and penalties or big money are involved, the losers in the cases sometimes request a review by one of California's six district **courts of appeal**. As appellate bodies, these courts do not hold trials. Lawyers make arguments and submit written briefs to panels of three justices, who decide whether the original trial was conducted fairly. These justices consider only possible legal errors, not the verdict in the case. If they find errors, they can send the case back for another trial or even dismiss the charges.

Ultimately, parties to the cases may petition for review by the seven-member state **supreme court**, the top of California's judicial ladder. Few cases reach this level because most are resolved in the lower courts and the high court declines most petitions. When the California Supreme Court hears a case, its decision is final unless issues of federal law or the U.S. Constitution arise; federal courts may consider such cases separately. Cases that involve only federal law or the U.S. Constitution start in federal district courts and may be appealed to federal appellate courts and the U.S. Supreme Court.

If a higher court refuses an appeal, the lower court's decision stands. Even when a case is accepted, the justices of the higher court have agreed only to consider the issues. They may or may not overturn the decision of the lower court.

Judicial Election and Selection

Although the tiered structure of the California courts is similar to that of the federal courts, the selection of judges is not. Federal judges and members of the U.S. Supreme Court are appointed by the president subject to confirmation by

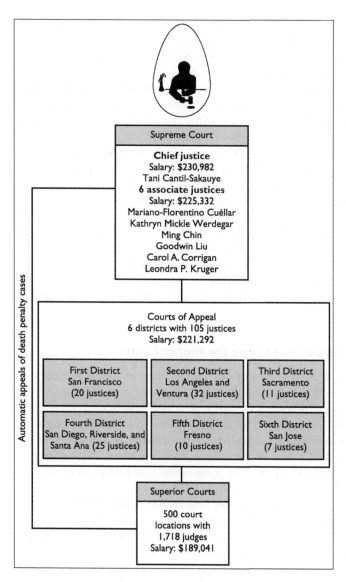

FIGURE 6.1 California Court System.

SOURCE: California Judicial Council.

the U.S. Senate. Once appointed, they serve for life. California judges and justices, however, gain office through a different process and regularly face the voters. This periodic scrutiny by the public, the media, and interest groups helps keep judges and their decisions in the news.

Formal qualifications to become a judge are minimal: candidates must have been admitted to practice law in California for at least ten years. Technically, superior court judges are elected, but most actually gain office initially through appointment by the governor when a sitting judge dies, retires, or is promoted between elections or sometimes when the legislature creates new judgeships. A governor who is elected to two terms of office may appoint as many as half of the state's sitting judges by the end of his or her second term, significantly affecting judicial practices. Governors generally appoint judges who are members of their own political parties, although Republican Governor **Arnold Schwarzenegger** was more willing than any other governor to appoint judges who were not members of his party. Prior service as a district attorney (prosecutor) has been common for successful appointees—a fact leading to complaints that judges are biased against defendants and defense attorneys. Governor **Jerry Brown**, however, has appointed several judges who have had experience as defense attorneys.

Appointed judges must run for office when their terms expire, but they almost always win because they're running as incumbents and often are unopposed. Of course, attorneys can become superior court judges by declaring their candidacy for a specific judicial office—usually when there is a vacancy due to retirement—and then running. In contested races, if no candidate wins a majority in the primary election, the two candidates with the most votes face each other in a **runoff election** in November. Superior court judges serve six-year terms and then may run for reelection, usually without opposition. Judges have no term limits.

Appointments and the Higher Courts

Unlike lower court judges, members of the district courts of appeal and the state supreme court attain office only by gubernatorial appointment. The governor's prospective nominees are screened by the state's legal community through its Commission on Judicial Nominees Evaluation. Then the nominees must be approved by the **Commission on Judicial Appointments**, consisting of the attorney general, the chief justice of the state supreme court, and the senior presiding justice of the courts of appeal. The commission may reject a nominee, but it has done so only twice since its creation in 1934.

Once approved by the Commission on Judicial Appointments, the new justices take office, but must go before the voters at the next gubernatorial election. No opponents or political party labels appear on the ballot; the voters simply check yes or no on the retention of the justices in question. If approved, they serve the remainder of the twelve-year term of the person they have replaced, at which time they can seek voter confirmation for a standard twelve-year term and additional terms after that—with no term limits.

Eleven other states select their supreme court justices in a similar fashion, but twenty-six rely solely on elections. The governor or legislature appoint justices in the remaining states.

Firing Judges

Almost all judges easily win election and reelection, mostly without opposition. Those who designed the system probably intended it to work this way. They wanted to distance judges somewhat from politics and to ensure their independence by giving them relatively long terms, thus also ensuring relatively consistent interpretation of the law. Avoiding costly election campaigns that depend on financial contributors also promotes independence. The framers of the U.S. Constitution put such a high value on judicial continuity and independence that they provided for selection by appointment rather than by election and allowed judges to serve for life. These values also seem well entrenched in California's political culture. But while the state's judges generally function without much criticism or interference, California's constitution provides several mechanisms of judicial accountability. Judges can be removed through elections, and they can be reprimanded or removed by a process within the judicial system.

Incumbent justices of the California Supreme Court routinely win reelection without serious challenge. In the 1970s and 1980s, however, both high court justices and superior court judges faced challenges from critics of decisions that supported racial integration or were seen as lenient toward criminals. Voters rejected some superior court judges, and in 1986, three liberal supreme court justices appointed by Jerry Brown during his first term as governor were swept out of office—the only justices removed by the voters in California history.

Judges in the superior (but not the appellate) courts may lose their jobs when a challenger runs against them and wins, although this is rare. Under California's system of direct democracy, judges can also be recalled (see Chapter 2). Only one California judge has ever been recalled (in 1913), but in 2016, a sentence many viewed as overly lenient in a rape trial in Santa Clara County resulted in an effort to recall the presiding judge.

The **Commission on Judicial Performance**, which investigates charges of misconduct or incompetence, may also remove judges. Commission members include three judges (appointed by the supreme court), two lawyers (appointed by the governor), and six public members (two each appointed by the governor, the senate Rules Committee, and the speaker of the assembly). Few investigations result in any action, but if the charges are confirmed, the commission may impose censure, removal from office, or forced retirement.

In 2014, forty-three judges were disciplined by the commission and in 2015, 1,245 complaints against judges were filed and 152 were investigated.[1] In the few cases in which the commission finds a judge to be at fault, it issues a warning or reprimand. For example, in 2014, two judges were censured for having sex in their chambers. Even more rarely, the commission may remove a judge from the bench. In recent years, judges have been removed for lying about campaign funds, threatening a district attorney, inappropriate interventions in trials, and excessive delays. Actual removals from the bench are rare, however, because those whose conduct is questionable usually resign before the commission's investigation is completed.

THE COURTS AT WORK

In 2013–2014, 7.5 million cases were filed in California's trial courts. Traffic infractions made up 65 percent of these cases. Criminal cases numbered 1,188,178

(16 percent), and the rest were civil suits (such as liability or contract disputes or small claims), divorce, juvenile, or family law cases.[2]

California's constitution guarantees the right to a jury trial for both criminal and civil cases; if both parties agree, however, a judge alone hears the case. In jury trials, prospective jurors are drawn from lists of licensed drivers, voters, and property owners, but finding a twelve-member jury is often difficult. Many people avoid jury duty because it takes time away from work and pays only a few dollars a day. Homemakers and retired people are most readily available, but they alone cannot make up a balanced jury. Poor people and minorities tend to be underrepresented because they are less likely to be on the lists from which jurors are drawn and because some avoid participation in a system that they distrust.

The parties in civil cases provide their own lawyers, although legal aid organizations sometimes help those who can't afford counsel. In criminal cases, the **district attorney**, an elected county official, carries out the prosecution. Defendants hire their own attorneys or are provided with court-appointed attorneys if they cannot afford one. California's larger counties employ a **public defender** to provide such assistance. Well over half of all felony defendants require court-appointed help.

Most cases never go to trial, though. Nearly 98 percent of all criminal cases are settled out of court, mostly when the defendant pleads guilty and **plea bargaining** produces a pretrial agreement on a plea and a penalty. Plea bargaining reduces the heavy workload of the courts and guarantees some punishment or restitution, but it also allows those charged with a crime to serve shorter sentences than they might have received if convicted of all charges. Most civil suits are also settled without a trial because the parties to the cases reach an agreement to avoid the high costs and long delays of a trial. Only about 0.2 percent of all cases are tried before a jury (9,900 in 2013–2014); a judge alone hears the others that go to trial.[3]

Notably, the judicial system as a whole—including judges, prosecutors, public defenders, lawyers, and juries—does not reflect the diversity of California's people. About 79 percent of California's 187,637 active attorneys are non-Hispanic whites, even though ethnic and racial minorities make up 60 percent of the population. About 40 percent of the state's attorneys are women, however—a number that is quickly rising.[4] Ethnic representation among California's judges is similar: 67 percent are male, and 69 percent are white.[5] These numbers lead critics to express concern about the fact that a predominantly white judicial system metes out justice to defendants who are, in the majority, nonwhite, and that punishment is less severe for whites than for minorities convicted of the same crime.[6] African Americans and Latinos perceive this situation and express deep mistrust of the system. Minority participation as attorneys and court officials has increased over time (Table 6.1 shows increasing diversity in judicial appointments), but considerable disparities remain.

Appeals

When a dispute arises over a trial proceeding or its outcome, the losing party may ask the appellate court or ultimately the supreme court to review the case.

T A B L E 6.1 Judicial Appointments by California Governors, 1959–2015

	Male	Female	White	Black	Hispanic	Asian
Ronald Reagan (R), 1967–1975	97.4% (478)	2.6% (13)	93.1% (457)	2.6% (13)	3.3% (16)	1.0% (5)
Jerry Brown (D), 1975–1983	84.0 (691)	16.0 (132)	75.5 (621)	10.9 (90)	9.4 (77)	4.3 (35)
George Deukmejian (R), 1983–1991	84.8 (821)	15.2 (147)	87.7 (849)	3.6 (35)	5.0 (49)	3.6 (35)
Pete Wilson (R), 1991–1998	74.6 (517)	25.4 (176)	84.4 (585)	5.2 (36)	4.9 (34)	5.5 (38)
Gray Davis (D), 1999–2003	65.8 (237)	34.2 (123)	70.8 (255)	9.25 (33)	12.8 (46)	7.2 (26)
Arnold Schwarzenegger (R), 2003–2010	65.0 (370)	35.0 (199)	73.7 (419)	7.6 (43)	10.7 (61)	8.0 (46)
Jerry Brown (D), 2011–2015*	61.7 (191)	38.3 (119)	60.8 (189)	11.6 (36)	15.8 (49)	8.7 (27)

*Racial percentages for Governor Brown's 2011–2015 appointees do not add up to 100 because 3 percent were in a new "Other" category.
SOURCE: Governor's Office.

Most appeals are refused, but the higher courts may agree to hear a case because of previous procedural problems (for instance, if the defendant was not read his or her rights) or because it raises untested legal issues. Appellate courts do not retry the case or review the facts in evidence; their job is to determine whether the original trial was fair and the law was applied appropriately. In addition to traditional appellate cases, the state supreme court automatically reviews all death penalty decisions. Although fewer than twenty a year, these cases take up a substantial amount of the supreme court's time. Neither the courts of appeal nor the state supreme court can initiate cases. No matter how eager they may be to intervene in an issue, they have to wait for someone else to bring the case to them.

Every year, about 8,000 petitions are filed with the California Supreme Court, mostly requesting reviews of cases decided by the courts of appeal. Each year, the members of the court, meeting "in conference" (that is, with no one else in attendance), choose about 200 petitions for consideration, a task that consumes an estimated 40 percent of the court's time. By refusing to hear a case, the court allows the preceding decision to stand. When the court grants a hearing, one of the justices (or a staff member) writes a "calendar memo" analyzing the case. Attorneys representing the two sides present written briefs and then oral arguments, during which they face rigorous questioning by the justices.

After hearing the oral arguments, the justices discuss the case in conference and vote in order of seniority; the chief justice casts the final, and sometimes decisive, vote. If the chief justice agrees with the majority, he or she assigns a justice to write the official court opinion; usually this is the same justice who wrote the initial calendar memo. A draft of the opinion then circulates among the justices, each of whom may concur, suggest changes, or write a dissenting opinion. Finally, after many months, the court's decision is made public. The California Supreme Court issued eighty-five opinions in 2013–2014—about 1 percent of all the petitions filed.

This time-consuming process allows plenty of room for politicking among the justices and depends on a high degree of cooperation and deferential behavior among them—what judges call **collegiality**—as a way of building consensus. With seven independent minds on the court, ongoing negotiations are needed to reach a majority and a decision.[7]

Managing the Courts

Besides leading the court through its decision making, the chief justice is responsible for managing the entire California court system and serves as chair of the **Judicial Council**, an appointed body of judges, attorneys, and legislators. The Judicial Council makes the rules for court procedures, collects data on the operations and workload of the courts, and oversees the administrative staff for the courts. The budget for the courts is set through the political process by the governor and the legislature, and the courts suffered budget cuts in recent years, resulting in complaints from leaders of the judiciary about heavier caseloads and longer waits for trials as well as political battles within the court system over whether to cut administrative or trial court costs. The 2016–2017 state budget provided new funding, however, including money to increase the number of judges.

THE HIGH COURT AS A POLITICAL BATTLEGROUND

The courts are especially important and powerful in California because of the nature of the state's political system. California's constitution has been amended over 500 times since it was written in 1879, making it both long and elaborately specific, with components addressing all sorts of matters, both major and mundane —and its density is constantly increased by initiatives. The length, detail, and continually changing complexity of California's constitution enhance the power of the state courts because their job is to determine whether laws and public policy are consistent with the constitution. California's practice of direct democracy adds to the workload of the courts because many initiatives are poorly drafted and many are challenged in the courts at some point. One scholar called the California courts a "shadow government"[8] because of their importance in shaping public policy; others view this as the courts' appropriate constitutional role.

The state supreme court is the ultimate interpreter of the state constitution (unless issues arise under the U.S. Constitution). The court's power makes it a center of political interest: governors strive to appoint justices who share their values and choose their appointees carefully. As governors have changed, so have the sorts of justices they appoint. And as the justices change, so does the political balance on the court, making it more conservative or liberal in its outlook.

Regardless of its collective political values, the court has not backed away from controversial issues, including occasionally overturning decisions of the legislature or the people (as expressed in initiatives). This willingness is less because of inter-ventionist attitudes on the part of the justices than because of a long, complex, and frequently amended constitution and poorly written laws and initiatives.

Governors, Voters, and the Courts

Long dominated by liberals, California's supreme court took a distinct turn toward the right in 1986, after the voters rejected the reelections of three liberal justices.

Appointed in 1977 by then-Governor Jerry Brown, the liberal justices waded into controversy with unpopular rulings on busing for school desegrega-tion and **Proposition 13** (the popular property tax reduction initiative), as well as consistently reversing death sentences even as public concern about crime increased. When three justices were on the ballot in 1986, conservative Repub-lican Governor George Deukmejian led a successful campaign to defeat them. With three new openings, Deukmejian transformed the court with conservative appointees, including a new chief justice.

Subsequent appointees by Republican governors maintained a conservative majority, but today more liberals sit on the court than at any time since 1986 because of recent appointments by Governor Jerry Brown. Today's court includes Kathryn Werdegar and Ming Chin (appointed by Republican Governor Pete Wilson) and Carol A. Corrigan and Chief Justice **Tani Cantil-Sakauye** (both appointed by Governor Arnold Schwarzenegger). The newest members of the court are Gordon Liu, Mariano-Florentino Cuéllar, and Leondra Kruger (all appointed by Governor Brown and relatively young, so they'll be on the court long after he's gone). Minority members of the court include Cantil-Sakauye (who is Filipina), Liu and Chin (who are Chinese), Cuéllar (who is Latino), and Kruger (who is African American). Three of the court's seven mem-bers are women. Except for Kruger, who will go before the voters in 2018, all of the current justices have won voter approval, with 65 to 75 percent voting for their retention.

Until Brown's appointees joined the court, the Republican-appointed majority was moderately conservative and less controversial than in the past. The court's conservatism was reflected in its tendency to be pro-prosecution in criminal cases and pro-business in economic cases. The court also disappointed local governments seeking new taxes with rulings that rigidly applied a requirement for two-thirds voter approval, a strict interpretation of 1978's **Proposition 13** (see Chapter 8), and in a 2011 ruling upholding the right of the state to dissolve local redevelop-ment agencies (as proposed by Governor Brown).

Overall, the supreme court has avoided **judicial activism** (making policy through court decisions rather than through the legislative or electoral process), but even the conservative-dominated court sometimes asserted its independence, wading into political controversy and significantly affecting state politics. In 2011, the Republican-dominated court rejected an appeal by the state Republican Party to overturn the legislative districts designed by the voter-created Citizens Redistricting Commission (see Chapter 5), upholding the work of the commission. And in 2014, the court ruled in favor of proceeding with the state's high-speed rail project, despite conservative opposition. Controversial cases often result in a split between the liberal and conservative wings of the court, but in 2016, when teacher tenure was challenged on grounds that it caused incompetent teachers to be routed to schools in poor neighborhoods, the court declined to hear the case, letting teacher tenure stand. The majority was composed of three conservatives and a liberal, and the dissenters—who wanted to take up the case—included two liberals and a conservative.

Most controversially, the courts sometimes overrule decisions of the voters, as the state supreme court did in its 2008 ruling on same-sex marriage. When the City and County of San Francisco licensed such marriages in 2004, the court ruled the marriages illegal on the basis of a 2002 law approved by voters through the initiative process. But the constitutionality of that law was challenged in 2008, and on a four-to-three vote, the conservative-dominated court ruled that "the California Constitution properly must be interpreted to guarantee this basic civil right to all Californians, whether gay or heterosexual, and to same-sex couples as well as to opposite-sex couples."[9] Opponents quickly qualified an initiative constitutional amendment for the ballot restricting marriage to opposite-sex couples. **Proposition 8** was approved by the voters, thus overruling the court. The initiative was challenged in court, but the California Supreme Court accepted it as a legitimate amendment to the state constitution. Then–Chief Justice **Ronald George** wrote that the court's decision was not based on whether Proposition 8 "is wise or sound as a matter of policy," but rather "concerns the right of the people ... to change or alter the state constitution itself.... Regardless of our views as individuals on this question of policy, we recognize as judges and as a court our responsibility to confine our consideration to a determination of the constitutional validity and legal effect of the measure in question."[10]

This decision did not put the issue to rest, however. The federal courts are sometimes drawn into battles over California initiatives, too. Since the 1990s, federal courts have overturned initiatives on campaign finance, open primary elections, and limits on public services for immigrants as violations of the U.S. Constitution, which trumps any state law or state constitution. In 2010, proponents of same-sex marriage took their case to a federal district court, arguing that Proposition 8 constituted a denial of equal rights under the U.S. Constitution. The judge in that case agreed, thus overriding both the voters of the state of California and the state supreme court. In 2012, this decision was appealed to the U.S. Supreme Court, which sustained the lower court on grounds that those arguing for Proposition 8 had no standing in the case because they could show no harm to themselves from same-sex marriage. In other words, the court avoided a ruling on the constitutionality of the law and rejected the case on a technicality. Same-sex marriages in California resumed on June 28, 2013.

Judicial rulings against voter-approved laws may seem undemocratic, but when the courts find an act of another branch of government or of the voters to be contrary to existing law or to the state or federal constitution, it is their responsibility to overturn that law, even if their decision is unpopular. "When we invalidate one of these initiatives," former Chief Justice George argued, "what we are doing is not thwarting the public's will. We are adhering to the ultimate expression of the popular will: the Constitution of the United States, or the Constitution of the State of California, which has been adopted by the people and which imposes limits on the initiative process and on lawmaking by legislatures and by the executive."[11]

Despite occasional controversial and hotly disputed decisions, the influence of the California Supreme Court goes well beyond this state. A study of court decisions throughout the country found that courts in other states followed precedents set in California more than those set in the courts of any other state.[12] This suggests that the California court is not only well within the mainstream of jurisprudence in the United States; it's a leader. It's also one reason why the court battle over same-sex marriages was so hard fought.

COURTS AND THE POLITICS OF CRIME

Crime topped the list of voter concerns in California and the nation during much of the 1980s and 1990s. Murder, rape, burglary, gang wars, and random violence seemed all too common. Republicans were elected governor at least partly because they were seen as law-and-order candidates.

Capital punishment was a key issue in the 1980s, when the liberal state supreme court overturned the vast majority of the death penalty cases it reviewed. Since 1986, when the voters rejected the liberal justices, the supreme court has affirmed most death sentences. The issue has not gone away, however. Law-and-order advocates condemn the lengthy and costly delays that plague death penalty appeals—up to ten years in state courts and another ten years in federal courts—but experts say that much of the delay is caused by the inability of the courts to find legal counsel for the condemned. Meanwhile, forensic methods such as DNA testing have revealed wrongful convictions in death penalty cases, and equal justice campaigners have noted that blacks are disproportionally condemned to death in relation to their proportion of the population.

Over 700 condemned murderers are on death row, and none has been executed since 2006, when the federal courts suspended executions in California because of concerns about the drugs used for lethal injections and the conditions of outdated facilities for executions. Former Chief Justice Ronald George, a supporter of the death penalty, called the system "dysfunctional" and said "a death row inmate in California is more likely to die of old age than by execution."[13] His successor, Chief Justice Cantil-Sakauye, has said the death penalty is "not effective."[14] In 2014, a federal judge took the argument one step further by overturning the death sentence of a convicted murderer on the grounds that California's long delays in implementing the sentence violated the "cruel and unusual punishment" clause of the Eighth Amendment of the U.S. Constitution.

The voters have chimed in, too, narrowly rejecting an initiative that would have banned the death penalty in 2012 on grounds that it constituted "cruel and unusual punishment" and that it actually costs more than life imprisonment. Opponents of the death penalty tried again in 2016, but lost again as voters approved an alternative initiative to retain the death penalty but speed up judicial review.

The law-and-order movement of the 1980s and 1990s also produced a series of propositions that strengthened penalties for many crimes, including the "three-strikes" initiative in 1994. Reflecting the view that liberal judges who were "soft on crime" were letting criminals off with light sentences, **"three strikes"** required anyone convicted of three felonies to serve a sentence of twenty-five years to life: "three strikes and you're out."

The three-strikes law quickly increased the state's prison population, as well as spending on prisons. The crime rate also declined, but violent crime peaked in 1992, two years before the three-strikes law, and it has continued to decline since then. In 2014, the crime rate was at its lowest since the 1960s,[15] although 2015 saw a small uptick in the rate. Conservatives attribute the decline to tougher judges and penalties, but many experts argue that the declining crime rate was due to economic prosperity and demographics, with fewer people in the age group most commonly associated with criminal activity. Even during the Great Recession, crime rates continued to decline. With crime less of a worry and concerns that the three-strikes law was too tough when the third strike was a minor crime, voters approved a 2012 ballot measure restricting third-strike penalties to violent crimes.

Meanwhile, the prison population in California is huge, which means the cost of incarcerating all these men and women is also huge. But despite a massive investment of tax funds, California's prisons are overcrowded and beset by violence and disease. A system built for 84,271 inmates housed 173,479 in 2006 (a historic high). Conditions were so bad that various inmate class action lawsuits have been in the federal courts since 2001. Eventually, a federal judge declared that conditions in California prisons constituted "cruel and unusual punishment" under the U.S. Constitution. When conditions hadn't improved sufficiently by 2009, federal judges ordered the state to come up with a plan to reduce the prison population. The state appealed to the U.S. Supreme Court, but in 2011 the court ruled against the state and ordered a substantial reduction in prison population within two years on grounds that overcrowding and health concerns violated the U.S. Constitution. Governor Brown responded by transferring lesser, nonviolent offenders from prisons to county jails. Designated **realignment**, this system reduced the population in state prison to 128,620 in 2016 and reduced costs, since jails are cheaper to operate, but it also imposed new responsibilities and costs on local governments (see Chapter 9).[16] The courts subsequently approved returning control of the prison health system to the state.

CALIFORNIA LAW

From crime to same-sex marriage, the issues discussed in this chapter remind us that the courts—both state and federal—play a central role in California politics. Controversies about judicial appointments and decisions make the political nature of the courts apparent, especially when the rulings of the court conflict with the will of the electorate as expressed in initiatives. Yet the courts can never be free of politics. They make policy by interpreting the law, and their judgments vary with the values of those who make them.

NOTES

1. "State Disciplined 43 Judges in 2014," *Los Angeles Times*, April 5, 2014; and State of California Commission on Judicial Performance, *2015 Annual Report*, http://cjp.ca .gov/res/docs/annual_reports/2015_Annual_Report.pdf (accessed November 5, 2016).

2. Judicial Council of California, *2015 Court Statistics Report*, www.courts.ca.gov (accessed June 27, 2016).

3. *Ibid.*

4. "Member Demographics" and "Predominantly White Male State Bar Changing ... Slowly," *California Bar Journal*, 2016 and 2012, www.calbarjournal.com (accessed June 29, 2016).

5. "Demographic Data Provided by Justices and Judges as of December 31, 2015," http://www.courts.ca.gov/documents/2016-Demographic-Report.pdf (accessed November 5, 2016).

6. See Lawyers' Committee for Civil Rights, www.lccr.com; or American Civil Liberties Union of Northern California, www.aclunc.org.

7. See Preble Stolz, Gerald F. Uelmen, and Susan Rasky, "The California Supreme Court," in *Governing California*, 2nd ed., edited by Gerald C. Lubenow. Berkeley: Berkeley Public Policy Press, Institute of Governmental Studies, University of California, 2006.

8. Charles Price, "Shadow Government," *California Journal*, October 1997, p. 38.

9. *In re Marriage Cases*, S147999.

10. *Ibid.*

11. Ronald George, "Promoting Judicial Independence," *Commonwealth*, February 2006, p. 10.

12. Jake Dear and Edward W. Jesson, "Followed Rates and Leading Cases, 1940–2005," *University of California, Davis, Law Review* 41 (April 2007): 683.

13. Ronald M. George, *Chief: The Quest for Justice in California*. Berkeley: Public Policy Press, Institute of Governmental Studies, University of California, 2013, pp. 7, 523.

14. "Top Judge Casts Doubt on Capital Punishment," *Los Angeles Times*, December 24, 2011.

15. "Open Justice," California Department of Justice, https://openjustice.doj.ca.gov /crimes/overview (accessed November 5, 2016).

16. For data on prisons, see Department of Corrections, "Population Reports," http://www.cdcr.ca.gov/Reports_Research/Offender_Information_Services_Branch/Population_Reports.html (accessed November 5, 2016). For an overview of the system, see *California's Future: Corrections*, Public Policy Institute of California, www.ppic.org (accessed July 1, 2016).

LEARN MORE ON THE WEB

For more on California's court system:
www.courts.ca.gov
www.ballotpedia.org/California_Supreme_Court

Information about attorneys is available from the State Bar of California:
www.calbar.org

For data on prisons, see California Department of Corrections and Rehabilitation:
www.cdcr.ca.gov

GET INVOLVED

You can learn about law and the courts through the Justice Corps, an AmeriCorps service-learning program with some compensation: go to http://www.courts.ca.gov/justicecorps.htm. You could also contact your county's district attorney or public defender or a local judge about an internship, although they generally prefer students who are in law school. Any of these will give you insights into how the courts and the law work at a local, personal level.

7

The Executive Branch: Coping with Fragmented Authority

LEARNING OBJECTIVES

7.1   Understand the governor: first among equals.

7.2   Differentiate the members of the supporting cast.

7.3   Examine the bureaucracy.

7.4   Describe how the pieces of the executive branch fit.

In American government, the executive branch has a rather clean look. Only the president and vice president are elected by the voters, albeit indirectly; leaders of the cabinet and most major posts within the branch are appointed by the chief executive, with many subject to confirmation by the U.S. Senate. The organization of the executive branch in most states stands in stark contrast to the national model. In fact, most states elect several members to executive branch positions in addition to the governor and lieutenant governor. In one case, North Dakota, voters choose ten executive branch officials in addition to the governor. At the other extreme, Arizona has only two elected executive branch positions along with the governor.

Of the fifty states, California has one of the larger executive branches. Along with a governor, the state's executive branch also includes a lieutenant governor, an attorney general, a secretary of state, a controller, a treasurer, an insurance commissioner, a superintendent of public instruction, and a five-member Board of Equalization. All are elected at the same time and serve four-year terms.

California also differs from the national executive branch in the way its executive branch officers are selected. Unlike the president and vice president, who are elected on the same political party ticket, each of these officeholders runs independently. The result is a cluttered branch of state government with

95

competing sources of power that often produce jurisdictional fragmentation. These schisms generate political stalemate or conflicts in the courts, and most of all confusion among the electorate. Thus, the California executive branch is anything but a unified governmental body.

THE GOVERNOR: FIRST AMONG EQUALS

The **governor** is California's most powerful public official. He or she shapes the state budget, appoints key policy makers in the executive and judicial branches, and both responds to and shapes public opinion on controversial issues. The governor also is the state's chief administrator; the unofficial leader of his or her political party; and liaison to other states, the U.S. government, and other nations. On occasion, the governor's powers extend even to international issues such as immigration or global warming.

The current governor of California, Democrat **Edmund G. ("Jerry") Brown, Jr.**, was reelected in 2014 after defeating Republican Neel Kashkari, formerly assistant treasury secretary under President George W. Bush (see Table 7.1). With an annual salary of $190,100, the office ranks second among the highest paid chief executives of the fifty states. In fact, the governor's salary is well below the incomes earned by many other government employees in California, particularly in large cities and counties, as well as judges, and many administrators at the University of California and California State University campuses. Other state employees such as prison wardens, retirement program coordinators, and physicians earn considerably more than the governor.

Jerry Brown's election to the governor's office is the latest example of California's bizarre politics. A political fixture in the state since his first election to the Los Angeles Community College District Board of Trustees in 1969 (that's not a typo!), Brown was elected governor in 1974 and 1978 after serving as the secretary of state. His father, Edmund G. ("Pat") Brown, also was elected governor in 1958 and 1962. Because his governorship occurred before California adopted term limits in 1990, Jerry Brown was eligible to run again. By the time he was halfway through his third term, Brown became the longest serving governor in California history. As long as term limits remain, Brown's tenure record will be preserved.

Formal Powers

Much of the governor's authority comes from formal powers written into the state's constitution and its laws. These responsibilities guide his or her relationships with the legislative and judicial branches, as well as with the other officeholders in the executive branch.

Submission of an Annual Budget.   No formal power is more important than the governor's budgetary responsibilities. The state constitution requires the governor to recommend a balanced budget to the legislature within the first ten days

T A B L E 7.1 California Governors and Their Parties, 1943–2019

Name	Party	Dates in Office
Earl Warren	Republican*	1943–1953
Goodwin J. Knight	Republican	1953–1959
Edmund G. Brown, Sr.	Democrat	1959–1967
Ronald Reagan	Republican	1967–1975
Jerry Brown	Democrat	1975–1983
George Deukmejian	Republican	1983–1991
Pete Wilson	Republican	1991–1999
Gray Davis	Democrat	1999–November 2003
Arnold Schwarzenegger	Republican	2003–2011
Jerry Brown	Democrat	2011–2019

*Warren cross-filed as both a Republican and a Democrat in 1946 and 1950.
SOURCE: California Secretary of State.

of each calendar year. The budget outlines the sources of state revenues and the recipients of state funds. Budget work is virtually a year-round task, consuming more of the governor's time than just about any other activity except emergencies such as earthquakes or fires. The governor is assisted in this effort by an appointed **director of finance**, who crafts the budget document after gathering data and funding requests from the dozens of departments and agencies within the state's bureaucracy. Initial preparations begin on July 1—the start of the fiscal year—and culminate with the governor's submission of a proposal to the legislature the following January (see Chapter 8). Officially, the process ends with the signing of the budget by the governor before the end of the fiscal year on June 30, so that the next year can begin with a budget in place.

Vetoes.   Under most circumstances, the governor has twelve days to act after the legislature passes a bill. On the hundreds of bills enacted by the legislature at a session's end, however, the governor has thirty days to act. Only a veto can keep a bill from becoming law. After the governor's time limit has passed, any unsigned or unvetoed bill becomes law the following January, along with the bills the governor has signed. If the bill is an urgency measure, it takes effect immediately upon signature.

When using the **general veto**, the governor rejects a bill in its entirety. This exercise of power can be overturned only by an absolute two-thirds vote in each chamber of the legislature, which rarely occurs. The governor has special powers on spending bills passed by the legislature, many of which are associated with the annual state budget. With spending bills, the governor cannot add money, but he or she can reduce or eliminate expenditures through use of the **item veto** before signing the budget into law. As with the general veto, an absolute two-thirds vote from each chamber is necessary to overturn item vetoes. Because of

T A B L E 7.2 Vetoes and Overrides, 1967–2014

Governor	Bills Vetoed (%)	Vetoes Overridden
Ronald Reagan (1967–1975)	7.3	1
Jerry Brown (1975–1983)	6.3	13
George Deukmejian (1983–1991)	15.1	0
Pete Wilson (1991–1999)	16.6	0
Gray Davis (1999–November 2003)	17.6	0
Arnold Schwarzenegger (November 2003–2011)	26.4	0
Jerry Brown (2011–2019)	13.3	0

SOURCE: Clerk, California State Senate.

that high threshold, legislators often attempt to head off vetoes by negotiating with the governor in advance.

Between 1982 and 2016, five successive governors exercised general and item vetoes without any repercussions from the legislature, and they did so with increasing frequency (see Table 7.2). More than any governor in history, Arnold Schwarzenegger turned the veto into a potent legislative weapon by rejecting more than one-fourth of the bills that reached his desk. The current governor, Jerry Brown, has used the veto more prudently. Ironically, the last time the legislature overturned a governor's veto was in 1979, when Jerry Brown was governor.

Special Session.   If the governor believes that the legislature has not addressed an important issue, he or she can take the dramatic step of calling a **special session**. At that time, the lawmakers must discuss only the specific business proposed by the governor. Special sessions often are called to respond to specific unmet needs, as when Governor Jerry Brown called the legislature into special session to pass legislation creating Covered California, the state's agency for the Patient Protection Affordable Care Act passed by Congress (also called Obamacare). The legislature obliged. But special sessions don't always produce their intended results. For example, in 2015, Brown called a special session to finance nearly $6 billion in unfunded needs for highways, roads, and bridges, which represented less than 10 percent of the state's backlog. In this case, the members could not reach agreement, leaving the state to suffer with one of the worst transportation networks in the nation. Brown has used special sessions relatively sparingly. His predecessor, Arnold Schwarzenegger, called sixteen special sessions during his seven years in office—the most of any governor in state history—leading some to believe that he had diluted the significance of the concept.[1]

Executive Order.   On occasion, the governor can make policy by signing an **executive order**, an action that looks similar to legislation. Governors must exercise this power carefully because such moves often lead to lawsuits over the breadth of their powers. Shortly after taking office in 2011, Jerry Brown signed several orders designed to curb state spending in the face of the state's huge $27 billion budget deficit. They included a state hiring freeze, drastic cutbacks on the purchase of state automobiles, and even the return of 48,000 cell phones used by state employees. In 2015, Brown responded to the state's four-year drought by ordering a 25 percent reduction from 400 hundred water supply agencies that served 90 percent of the state's residents. Said Brown, "People should realize we are in a different era.... The idea of your nice little green lawn getting water every day, those ideas are past."[2]

Appointment Powers.   Before the Progressive reforms, California governors used patronage, or the "spoils" system, to hire friends and political allies. Today, 99 percent of all state employees are selected through a civil service system based on merit, rather than patronage. Still, the governor fills about 2,500 key positions in the executive departments and cabinet agencies, except for the Departments of Justice and Education, whose top officials are elected by the voters. Together, these appointees direct the state bureaucracy (see Figure 7.1).

The state senate must approve most of the governor's appointees. Generally, senate confirmation is routine, but occasionally the governor's choice for a key post is rejected for reasons other than qualifications. In instances of an opening in the executive branch, both chambers of the legislature must weigh in with majority votes. In early 2010, Governor Schwarzenegger nominated Republican State Senator Abel Maldonado to fill the lieutenant governor vacancy resulting from Lieutenant Governor John Garamendi's election to a vacated congressional seat. Maldonado was confirmed, only to lose in the November 2010 general election to Democrat Gavin Newsom.

The governor also appoints people to more than 300 state boards and commissions. Membership on some boards—such as the Arts Council and the Commission on Aging, which have only advisory authority—is largely ceremonial and without pay. Other boards, however, such as the California Energy Commission (CEC), the Public Utilities Commission (PUC), the California Coastal Commission (CCC), and the California Air Resources Board (CARB), make important policies free from direct gubernatorial control. Nevertheless, the governor affects these "independent" boards through his or her appointments and manipulation of the budget.

Perhaps the most enduring of all gubernatorial appointments are judgeships. The governor fills both vacancies and new judgeships that are periodically created by the legislature. Most judges continue to serve long after those who appointed them have left office. However, the governor's power is checked to a degree by various judicial commissions and by the voters in future elections. Current Governor Jerry Brown has acknowledged the state's growing diversity by appointing high numbers of people of color and women to judicial posts.

In addition to the major areas of formal authority discussed earlier, the governor has a wide range of other formal powers. He or she is commander in chief of the California National Guard, which on occasion is sent to help manage local crises in the state on a short-term basis. The governor also can grant pardons, reprieves, or sentence commutations, although such authority is rarely exercised.

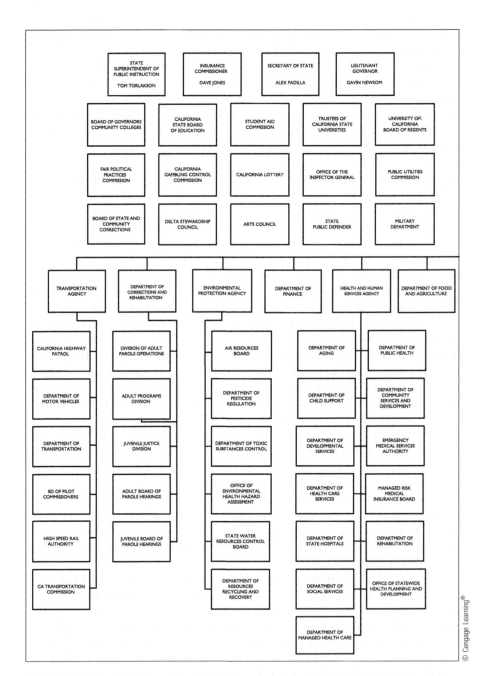

FIGURE 7.1 State Executive Branch Departments and Agencies, 2014, www.cold.ca .gov/Ca_State_Gov_Orgchart.pdf.

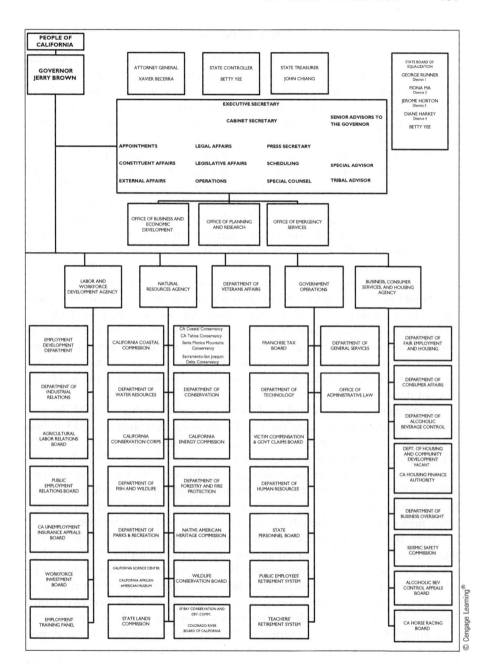

FIGURE 7.1   (Continued)

Finally, the governor is the ceremonial head of state for greeting dignitaries from other countries. Along with the other major functions, these powers keep the governor very active and in the public eye.

Informal Powers

Formal constraints on the governor can be offset to some extent by a power that is not written into the constitution at all, yet is effective nonetheless: the governor's popularity. When the governor stands in good stead with other legislators and/or the public, he or she is often able to overcome political opponents.

Historically, California's governors have used the prestige of their office to push their own agendas. During his tenure, Democratic Governor Gray Davis operated with a personality that left little room for disagreement. He attacked the other branches of state government, claiming that state legislators were supposed to implement his vision and that judicial appointees should reflect his views.[3] As he campaigned for reelection in 2002, the state suffered a perfect storm from exorbitant energy costs, a lengthy recession, and huge budget shortfalls. Despite his victory, the voters lost patience with Davis. In a July 2003 Field Poll, 61 percent of the respondents blamed Davis for the state's problems,[4] leading to an unprecedented successful recall effort in October 2003. Davis first lost his public support and informal power, and soon after that, his job.[5]

Arnold Schwarzenegger used his informal power to circumvent the legislature, whose members he called "girlie men" for not adopting his budgets.[6] Repeatedly, he cut deals directly with organizations and institutions from local governments to universities, prison guards' union, and Indian gaming interests. In 2010, Schwarzenegger negotiated pension reforms with several state employee unions that mandated higher employee contributions—something the legislature had not dared to even tackle.[7]

Schwarzenegger had mixed results with the voters. In March 2004, he successfully barnstormed the state for a ballot measure, described as a $15 billion "recovery" bond that temporarily balanced the state budget. But in 2005, Schwarzenegger suffered a stinging defeat, when voters rejected his ballot measures on teacher tenure, union campaign contributions, strict state budget controls, and legislative redistricting. His standing in public opinion polls plummeted from 64 percent approval to 35 percent in ten short months.[8] Schwarzenegger never fully recovered, although he managed to win reelection in 2006.

Jerry Brown has approached his current occupancy of the governorship much differently than his first go-around thirty-six years earlier. With his election in 2010 at the age of seventy-two, Brown became the oldest person to be elected to the position; coincidentally, when he was elected in 1974 at the age of thirty-six, he was the state's youngest since 1863. During his first two terms, Brown had a contentious relationship with the legislature. He was nicknamed "Governor Moonbeam" for a variety of futuristic and sometimes whimsical proposals thought by many to be couched in anything but reality.

That was then. Between stints in the governor's office, Brown was chair of the state Democratic party, served as mayor of Oakland, and was elected state attorney general. And he married. The combination of these experiences and more produced the transformation of Jerry Brown.

In his current stint, Brown has shown a blend of patience and quiet urgency with the legislature about solving the state's issues. He has assiduously courted

Democrats and Republicans, liberals and conservatives. His efforts notwithstanding, Brown has not been able to suture the differences within the legislature. As he recently lamented, "There's not a thread of common purpose" between the two sides.[9]

Still, Brown has persevered. He has battled with the legislature on the budget, going so far as to veto the entire document in 2011 before accepting a modified version (see Chapter 8 for budget issues). Elsewhere, in 2011, he convinced the legislature to pass his **realignment** plan to move nonviolent prisoners from state facilities to less expensive county jails. In 2012, he persuaded the legislature to spend most of a $10 billion bond on the first leg of the state's proposed high-speed rail system, despite skittish public opinion and uncertain future funds. In the same year, he helped narrow future state budget deficits by securing agreements from public employee unions on wage cuts of almost 5 percent and convinced the legislature to pass pension reforms. As the economy recovered in 2013 and 2014, Brown agreed to restore some of those cuts.

Perhaps Brown's biggest victory has come with the voters, not the state legislature. During his 2010 campaign, he promised never to raise taxes without voter approval. In 2012, he asked the voters to pass **Proposition 30**, officially entitled Temporary Taxes to Fund Education. The proposal called for raising income taxes for those earning $250,000 or more for seven years along with a statewide sales tax increase of 0.25 percent for four years. Despite near universal predictions of defeat, the voters approved Proposition 30 by eleven points. Now with an extra $7 billion flowing in for underfunded public education, Brown asked the legislature to pass the **Local Education Funding Formula**, a novel plan that provided extra education funds for poor students and English learners and increased local control of funds. The new funding source has received acclaim from teacher and education administrator organizations as well as parent groups—three sources who rarely agree on education policy.[10] Volatility in state revenues led Brown to endorse a twelve-year extension of Proposition 30 in 2016, and that measure passed in spite of an uncertain economy and other new tax measure proposals. The voters agreed.

Jerry Brown hasn't won all his battles, nor has he always pleased traditional allies. His efforts to move fresh water underneath the Delta through what he describes as "peripheral tunnels" have been derided by environmentalists as a threat to endangered species. His public pension reform legislation has been ridiculed by conservatives as little more than symbolic change. His veto of a bill that would have made it easier for farmworkers to organize drew the wrath of unions. And his unwillingness to devote more funds for the disabled has been criticized by social welfare advocates as unduly harsh. Nevertheless, he has enjoyed broad support in public opinion polls at levels far greater than approval of the legislature, and that backing has helped give the governor room to operate. In a 2016 Field Poll, voters approved Brown's performance by a margin of almost two to one.[11]

Ever-Changing Relationships

The powers of the governor's office remain basically the same year after year and administration after administration. But how those powers are managed depends on the issues, the times, the political environment, and the personality of the occupant. Yet one fact remains indisputable: the governor is clearly first among equals in the executive branch.

THE SUPPORTING CAST

Most states provide for the election of a lieutenant governor, a secretary of state, a treasurer, and an attorney general, but few elect an education officer, a controller, a Board of Equalization, or an insurance regulator. Moreover, most states require the governor and the lieutenant governor (and others, in some cases) to run on the same political party ticket, thus providing some cohesion. Not so in California, where each elected member of the executive branch is elected independently of the others.

The consequences can be quite serious. For example, when Governor Schwarzenegger unilaterally withheld $3.1 billion from the public schools in 2005 in defiance of what many believed were state guarantees, Superintendent of Public Instruction Jack O'Connell sued. Ultimately, O'Connell dropped the suit after the governor and public school officials found agreement. On another occasion, then–state insurance commissioner, Republican Steve Poizner, sued to stop the sale of the state-run workers' compensation insurance fund, proposed by fellow Republican Governor Arnold Schwarzenegger. The issue was dropped after Schwarzenegger and Poizner left office. These examples show the extent to which very public fights can occur between two independently operating officeholders in the executive branch.

Such acrimony was absent during Brown's terms, largely because Democrats controlled every statewide office as well as large majorities in the state legislature. Nevertheless, the potential for battles between elected executive branch officials is a constant.

The Lieutenant Governor

The **lieutenant governor** is basically an executive-in-waiting with few formal responsibilities. If the governor becomes disabled or is out of the state, the lieutenant governor fills in as acting governor. If the governor leaves office, the lieutenant governor takes over. This has happened seven times in the state's history, most recently in 1953, when **Goodwin Knight** replaced Earl Warren, who became chief justice of the U.S. Supreme Court. The current lieutenant governor, Democrat and former San Francisco mayor Gavin Newsom, was elected in 2010, displacing Abel Maldonado, who had been appointed to the office earlier in the year. Newsom was reelected in 2014.

The lieutenant governor heads some units, such as the State Lands Commission and the Commission on Economic Development, and is an *ex officio* (automatic, by virtue of the office) member of the University of California Board of Regents and California State University Board of Trustees. He or she also serves as president of the state senate, but this job, too, is long on title and short on substance. As senate president, the lieutenant governor may vote to break 20–20 ties, an event that last occurred in 1976. So minimal are the responsibilities of the lieutenant governor that one occupant once quipped that his biggest daily task was to wake up, check the morning newspaper to see whether the governor had died, and then return to bed![12] That description may stretch the point a bit, but not by much. As current Lieutenant Governor Newsom recently said about the office, "it's just so dull."[13] Still, Newsom has tried to bring life to the office (and his future run for governor in 2018) by sponsoring initiatives on the legalization of marijuana and tighter gun control laws in 2016.

The Attorney General

Despite the lieutenant governor's higher rank, the **attorney general** is usually considered the second-most powerful member of the executive branch. As head of the Department of Justice, the attorney general oversees law enforcement activities, acts as legal counsel to state agencies, represents the state in important cases, and renders opinions on (that is, interprets) proposed and existing laws. The attorney general also writes the titles and summaries of proposed initiatives, which sometimes stirs antagonism from initiative proponents or opponents—or both! In the 2014 contest for attorney general, incumbent Democrat **Kamala Harris** was reelected with little competition. Harris was also the first female and person of color to hold the post. When Harris was elected to fill the seat of retiring U.S. Senator Barbara Boxer in 2016, Governor Jerry Brown nominated, and the state legislature confirmed, U.S. Representative Xavier Becerra, a Democrat, to the Attorney General position for the remainder of the term.

Substantial authority and independent election allow the attorney general to chart a course separate from the governor on important state questions. Harris has done just that. In 2011, she rejected a $20 billion settlement of a suit accepted by forty-eight other states against five major banks for abusive practices, arguing that Californians would be shortchanged. A few months later, the banks agreed to $32 billion, enabling California to gain a much larger share of the disbursement.[14] Harris also emerged as a key advocate for gun control laws and took software developers to task on privacy issues.

The Secretary of State

Unlike the U.S. cabinet official who bears the same title, the **secretary of state** of California is basically a records keeper and elections supervisor. The job entails maintaining voter registration files; certifying the number and validity of signatures obtained for initiatives, referenda, and recall petitions; producing sample ballots and ballot arguments for the voters; publishing official election results; and keeping candidate campaign finance records. The current secretary of state, Democrat and former state senator **Alex Padilla**, was elected in 2014.

Recently, the secretary of state has looked into converting California's election system from paper ballots to electronic voting machines. However, former

Secretary of State Debra Bowen (2006–2014) resisted the change because of her concern that electronic voting machines were prone to viruses or manipulation. As a result, counties have been forced to either invest in new state-certified machines that include paper verification or resort to paper ballots. Secretary Padilla campaigned on modernizing the state's balloting process, but the electronic voting machine issue remains unresolved.

The Superintendent of Public Instruction

The **superintendent of public instruction** heads the Department of Education. He or she is the only elected official in the executive branch chosen by nonpartisan ballot. Unless one candidate wins a majority in the June primary, the top two candidates face each other in the November general election. The superintendent's powers are severely limited. Funding is determined largely by the governor's budgetary decisions, and policies are closely watched by the governor-appointed state board of education and the education committees of the legislature.

In general, the electorate knows little about the office, but teachers' unions, education administrators, education reform groups, and other affected groups take great interest in the position because this official advocates for California's massive public education system. The current superintendent of public instruction, former state senator and assemblyman **Tom Torlakson**, was elected in 2010 with strong support from the California Teachers' Association, the most powerful education organization in the state. He was reelected in 2014 after a bruising election fight with Marshall Tuck, who had campaigned for reforms that included stricter teacher accountability.

The Money Officers

Perhaps the most fractured part of the executive branch of California government lies with the elected officials who manage the state's money. Courtesy of the Progressive reformers who feared a concentration of power (see Chapter 1), the controller, the treasurer, and the Board of Equalization have separate but overlapping responsibilities in this area. The **controller** supervises all state and local tax collection and writes checks for the state, including those to state employees. The controller is also an *ex officio* member of several agencies, including the Board of Equalization, the Franchise Tax Board, and the State Lands Commission. Of all the "money officers," the controller is the most powerful, and thus the most prominent. The current controller, Democrat and former Board of Equalization member **Betty Yee**, was elected in 2014 in her first run for statewide office. Her campaign focused on bringing substantive tax reform to California.

The **treasurer** invests state funds raised through taxes and other means until they are needed for expenditures. The treasurer also borrows money for the state by issuing bonds approved by the voters. Typically amounting to several billion dollars, the bonds are sold in financial markets to permit development of long-term projects such as highways, water projects, or other infrastructure needs. The state then "redeems" the bonds over time through interest payments. In another case of political musical chairs (see Chapter 4), Democrat and termed-out State Controller **John Chiang** was elected to this office in 2014. In 2016, Chiang announced that he would seek the governorship in 2018.

The **Board of Equalization**, also part of California's fiscal system, oversees the collection of excise taxes on sales, gasoline, and liquor. The board also reviews county property assessment practices to ensure uniform calculation methods and practices. The board has five members—the controller, plus four who are elected in districts of equal population. Historically, the board has attracted little attention, but in 2007, the members voted to tax "alcopops"— sweet alcohol drinks often consumed by underage drinkers—at the same rate as hard liquor instead of beer. The change would have raised the tax from 20 cents per gallon to $3.30 per gallon, increasing the cost of alcopop drinks by about 25 percent, but manufacturers avoided the tax by lowering the alcohol content.

The Insurance Commissioner

The office of **insurance commissioner** exemplifies the persistent reform mentality of California voters. Until 1988, the office was part of the state's Business, Housing, and Transportation Agency. However, with soaring insurance rates, voters approved an initiative that called for 20 percent across-the-board reductions in automobile insurance premiums and created the elected position of insurance commissioner. Consumer Watchdog, the public interest group behind the proposition, claims that the law saved California drivers more than $102 billion during its first twenty-five years of existence.

Democrat **Dave Jones**, a termed-out member of the state assembly, was first elected to the office in 2010 and reelected in 2014. Jones campaigned with the promise to hold health insurance companies accountable for any rate increases, an authority not held by the commissioner. **Proposition 45** on the November 2014 ballot asked the voters to give such authority to the state insurance commissioner, but the initiative went down to defeat after a vigorous fight by the health insurance industry.

The Supporting Cast—Snow White's Seven Dwarfs?

Combined, the seven other elected members of the executive branch (plus the Board of Equalization) present an appearance of tremendous political activity. Still, their efforts often center on narrow policy areas and frequently are in opposition to one another, as well as to the much more powerful governor.

THE BUREAUCRACY

Elected officials are just the most observable part of the state's administrative machinery. Backing them up, implementing their programs, and dealing with citizens on a daily basis are about 228,000 state workers—the **bureaucracy**.

Only about 5,000 of these workers are appointed by the governor or by other executive officers. The remainder are hired and fired through the state's **civil service**. The Progressives designed this system to insulate government workers from political influences and to make them more professional than those who might be hired out of friendship.

The task of the bureaucracy is to carry out the programs established by the policy making institutions: the executive branch, the legislature, and the judiciary, along with a handful of regulatory agencies. However, because bureaucrats are permanent, full-time professionals, they sometimes influence the content of programs and policies, chiefly by advising public officials or by exercising the discretion built into the laws that define bureaucratic tasks. The bureaucracy can also influence policy through the lobbying efforts of its employee organizations (see Chapter 4).

State bureaucrats work for various departments and agencies (see Figure 7.1), each run by an administrator who is appointed by the governor and confirmed by the senate. Sometimes, political appointees and civil servants clash over the best ways to carry out state policy. If the bureaucracy becomes too independent, the governor can always use his or her budgetary powers to bring it back into line or, in some cases, dismiss appointees.

In recent years, California's bureaucrats have been particularly ambitious on climate change. The California Energy Commission (CEC) has instituted energy efficiency standards for televisions and other electrical appliances. Also, the California Air Resources Board (CARB) has led the way in regulating greenhouse gas levels. These efforts have kept California's energy consumption flat during the past three decades, compared with a 40 percent increase in energy consumption nationwide. They have also established California as a trendsetting state on the issues of global warming and energy use.

Some observers have criticized California's bureaucracy as unnecessarily inflated and unresponsive, even though the size of the state's system ranks forty-fifth of the fifty states on a per capita basis.[15] Still, there is no denying that slim or not, the state's bureaucracy grew under the Schwarzenegger administration to about 240,000, despite his promise to "blow up the boxes" of the bureaucracy shortly after taking office. Under Governor Jerry Brown, the size of the state bureaucracy has actually declined by more than 10,000 employees, as he and the legislature have struggled to find ways to reduce the cost of state government. Brown has also successfully promoted pension reform, which has curbed the state's obligations to future state government retirees.

MAKING THE PIECES FIT

The executive branch is a hodgepodge of independently elected authorities who serve in overlapping and conflicting institutional positions. Nobody, not even the governor, is really in charge. Each official simply attempts to carry out his or her mission with the hope that passable policy will result. Occasionally, reformers have suggested streamlining the system by consolidating functions and reducing the number of elective offices, but the only recent change has been the addition of yet another office, that of insurance commissioner.

Despite these obstacles, the officeholders—most notably governors—have been active policy makers. Pete Wilson waged war against illegal immigrants, affirmative action, and welfare while trumpeting "law and order." Gray Davis responded to the state's power shortage crisis. Arnold Schwarzenegger was instrumental in environmental reform. And Jerry Brown has championed efforts to deal with California's unpredictable water supply.

Still, the governor does not operate in a vacuum. He or she must contend with other members of the executive branch, a fractured and suspicious legislature, independent courts, a professional bureaucracy, and, most of all, an electorate with a highly erratic collective pulse. Whether these conditions are challenges or impediments, they make the executive branch a fascinating element of California government.

NOTES

1. "Special Sessions Define Schwarzenegger," *Sign on San Diego*, October 22, 2009, http://signonsandiego.printthis.clickability.com/pt/cpt?action=cpt&tit.

2. "California Imposes First Mandatory Water Restrictions to Deal with Drought," *New York Times*, April 1, 2015, www.nytimes.com/2015/04/02/us/california -imposes-first-ever-water-restrictions-to-deal-with-drought.html?_r=0.

3. See "Tensions Flare between Davis and His Democrats," *Los Angeles Times*, July 22, 1999, pp. A1, A28; and "Davis Comments Draw Fire," *San Jose Mercury News*, March 1, 2000, p. 14A.

4. *The Field Poll*, Release #2074, July 15, 2003.

5. For an account of how Davis fell from power, see Larry N. Gerston and Terry Christensen, *Recall! California's Political Earthquake*. Armonk, NY: M. E. Sharpe, 2004.

6. "Gov. Criticizes Legislators as 'Girlie Men'," *Los Angeles Times*, July 18, 2004, pp. B1, B18.

7. "Governor Slashes Workers' Pay," *San Francisco Chronicle*, July 2, 2010, pp. C1, C6.

8. "Schwarzenegger's Popularity Slide," *Los Angeles Times*, October 28, 2005, p. B2.

9. "Policymaking on Hold as Brown Nurses His Wounds," *Los Angeles Times*, August 17, 2011, pp. AA1, AA4.

10. "CTA, School Groups Back Brown's Latest Funding Regs," *Cabinet Report*, January 9, 2014, https://cabinetreport.com/politics-education/cta-school-groups -back-browns-latest-funding-regs.

11. "Voters Approve of Brown's Job Performance Nearly Two to One: More Think California Is Moving in the Right Direction," Field Poll, January 14, 2016, www .field.com/fieldpollonline/subscribers/Rls2527.pdf.

12. "The Most Invisible Job in Sacramento," *Los Angeles Times*, May 10, 1998, pp. A1, A20.

13. "Uh, Gavin...," *San Francisco Chronicle*, May 31, 2012, p. A15.

14. "Rising Star Mixes Idealism, Political Savvy," *San Francisco Chronicle*, April 29, 2012, pp. A1, A12.

15. "State and Local Government Employees: Where Does California Rank—2011 Update," September. Palo Alto, CA: Center for Continuing Study of the California Economy, 2012.

LEARN MORE ON THE WEB

Office of the Attorney General:
www.caag.state.ca.us

Office of the Governor:
www.gov.ca.gov

Office of the Secretary of State:
www.ss.ca.gov

Office of the State Board of Equalization:
www.boe.ca.gov

Office of the State Controller:
www.sco.ca.gov

Office of the State Insurance Commissioner:
www.insurance.ca.gov

Office of the State Superintendent of Public Instruction:
www.cde.ca.gov/eo

Office of the State Treasurer:
www.treasurer.ca.gov

Salaries of state employees:
www.capitolweekly.net/salaries/index.php?_c=yzbexjathf9ge0

GET INVOLVED

Determine whether the governor or any of the statewide elected officials has an office in your area. Ask if you can "shadow" the policy maker when he or she visits the local office. By doing so, you'll be able to learn how these officials interact with their constituents, fellow policy makers, and interest groups, as well as gain a greater understanding of the state bureaucracy. If there is no such office in your area, write a letter about a public policy concern and send it to the appropriate statewide official to see how he or she responds.

8

Taxing and Spending: Budgetary Politics and Policies

LEARNING OBJECTIVES

8.1 Describe California's budget environment.

8.2 Explain the budgetary process and players.

8.3 Trace revenue sources.

8.4 Compare spending categories.

8.5 Review California's budget: too little, too much, or just right?

The most fundamental task of government is to protect its citizens. At the state level, these services range from the obvious such as law enforcement, safe roads, and public schools to the less noticeable, including drinkable water, well-built structures, and disease prevention. But where does the government get the means to provide these and other services? Fundamentally, from taxes, fees, and other revenue sources.

The connection between taxing and spending is not always easy to see. Even though most people may agree on taxes in principle, they often disagree on how much should be collected and from whom, as well as the recipients of those funds. Occasionally, voters may defeat an elected official if he or she strays too far from the sentiments from his or her district. More dramatically, when policy makers as a group seem to drift from general public values on taxing and spending, the voters may resort to direct democracy to reorder the state's fiscal priorities. With so many more policy areas of need than dollars available, much is at stake.

CALIFORNIA'S BUDGET ENVIRONMENT

Unlike the national government, which usually operates with a deficit, state constitutions require balanced budgets. This has been difficult in California, where a steady flow of immigrants, a burgeoning school-aged population, massive incarceration rates, and deteriorating infrastructure present a challenging budget environment. Too often, unanticipated revenue deficits have punctured the state's capabilities to meet its needs. A $34 billion revenue hole helped seal the fate of Governor Gray Davis in an unprecedented 2003 recall election. Although his replacement, Arnold Schwarzenegger, promised fiscal soundness, deficits were more common than not during his seven years in office. In 2008, the state faced a $15 billion revenue shortfall, forcing drastic cuts. In 2009, Schwarzenegger and the legislature grappled with a massive $42 billion budget hole caused in part by the Great Recession. The very next year, the weary governor and legislature faced a new $21 billion deficit. Again, they cut.

On his return to the state's highest office in 2011, Jerry Brown found himself haunted by the same environment that had plagued his predecessors. This time, the state faced a $27 billion deficit for the coming fiscal year, leading to new cuts in almost every program area except prisons. By 2012, an exasperated Governor Brown and the legislature plugged half of a $16 billion hole for the coming fiscal year. But Brown warned there would be three fewer weeks in the school year unless the voters passed a November initiative, Proposition 30, which collected temporary tax increases of about $7 billion annually for seven years to generate the rest. They did.

Even so, California's state budget shriveled from about $105 billion in 2005–2006 to $91 billion in 2012–2013, as the state's population grew from 36 million to 38.6 million. Funding for schools placed California near the bottom on a per capita basis, while the gamut of social welfare programs and their recipients suffered mightily. The passage of Proposition 30 in 2012 and a recovering economy once again put the state on the right track. In 2016–2017, the state's budget grew to $122.2 billion for 39.2 million residents. Still, major issues have been left without resolution.

The voters haven't helped with this ongoing dilemma. Over the past quarter century, voters have passed a series of ballot propositions directing the state to spend money on various programs ranging from longer prison sentences to more comprehensive public education without providing the funds. On other occasions, voters have acknowledged a programmatic need, plave write but have been unwilling to pay for its solution. Consider state roads in California, where gasoline taxes have not been raised since 1992, even though automobiles get better mileage and use less fuel. A 2015 study found that 51 percent of California's roads were in poor condition, costing drivers more than $18 billion annually, or $762 per motorists—nearly twice the national average.[1] In a statewide survey conducted in the same year, two-thirds of the respondents agreed that roads were "a big problem" or "somewhat of a problem." Yet, when asked if they would approve a gasoline tax increase, only 18 percent said "yes."[2] This typifies the political environment in which elected officials must make tough decisions.

THE BUDGETARY PROCESS

Budget making is a complicated and lengthy activity in California that lasts almost an entire year. Participants include the governor and various executive-branch departments, the legislature, the public (via initiative and referendum), and, increasingly, the courts when judges uphold or overturn commitments made by the other policy makers.

The Governor and Other Executive Officers

Preparation of the annual budget is the governor's most important formal power; no other state public official has as much clout. The governor frames the document before it goes to the legislature, and then has additional say afterward through the item veto. Given this unique power position, legislative leaders often negotiate with the chief executive over what he or she will accept long before the budget lands on the governor's desk.

During the summer and fall, the governor's director of finance works closely with the heads of state agencies. Supported by a staff of fiscal experts and researchers, the director of finance gathers and assesses information about the anticipated needs of each department and submits a "first draft" budget to the governor in late fall. The governor presents a refined version of this draft to the legislature the following January. The state constitution gives the legislature until June 15 to respond.

Legislative Participants

Upon receiving the budget in January, the legislature's leaders refer the document to the legislative analyst. Over the next two months, the legislative analyst and his or her staff scrutinize each part of the budget, considering needs, costs, anticipated revenues, and other factors. Often, the analyst's findings clash with those of the governor.

Meanwhile, two key legislative units in each chamber—the appropriations committees and the budget committees—shepherd the budget proposal through the legislative process. After the staffs of these committees spend about two months analyzing the entire document, each chamber assigns portions to various committees and their staffs. During this time, lobbyists, individual citizens, government officials, and other legislators testify on the proposed budget before committees and subcommittees. By mid-April, the committees conclude their hearings, combine their portions into a single document, and bring the budget bill to their respective full house for a vote.

As June nears and the two chambers hone their versions, a select group of leaders enter into informal negotiations over the document. Known as the **Big Five**, the governor, the speaker of the assembly, the president pro tem of the senate, and the minority party leaders of each house become the nucleus of the final budgetary decisions. There have been exceptions. For example, during his most recent stint as governor, Jerry Brown has worked almost solely with Democratic legislative leaders, thanks to large Democratic majorities. Regardless, should the two chambers differ on specifics, the budget bill goes to a two-chamber conference committee for reconciliation, after which both chambers vote again. With passage of **Proposition 25** in 2010, it now takes a simple majority to pass the budget, a change from the previous long-standing two-thirds requirement. Ever since the proposition's approval, every state budget has been passed on time. However, because a two-thirds vote is still required for revenue increases, the significance of this change is questionable.

The Courts

Sometimes, the courts weigh in on key budget issues to address some of the "quick fixes" to complex budget issues enacted by public policy makers or the voters. In 2008, a decision by the U.S. District Court forced the state to spend billions of dollars on improved prison conditions, adding still more to a budget already billions of dollars in the red. Governor Schwarzenegger was humbled twice in 2010 when a state appeals court ruled that in an effort to balance the state budget, he could not furlough state workers. In 2011, a federal judge ordered the state to increase payments for foster parents because California's payment structure was out of compliance with federal law. And in 2014, a federal appeals court ruled that the state could not take away overtime pay for home care workers, something the Brown administration had imposed as another budget-fixing measure. Clearly, the courts have found reason to shape state budgets, particularly when the governor and legislators choose expediency over legality.

The Public

On occasion, the public shapes the budget through initiatives or referenda. The voters relied on ballot propositions to approve the sales tax (1933) and repeal the inheritance tax (1982). In 1993. the voters passed a proposition that increased the state sales tax by 0.5 percent, with new revenues exclusively earmarked for local public safety programs. In 2004, the voters enacted an initiative that created an additional 1 percent tax bracket for people with taxable incomes of $1 million or more, with the funds designated for mental health programs. And in 2012, the voters passed **Proposition 30**, which temporarily increased sales and income taxes for individuals with annual incomes over $250,000 to offset declining state revenues. Supporters proposed a twelve-year extension of the measure for income taxes only in 2016, and the voters agreed again, this time with the extra funds dedicated to public education and health care. In the same year, the voters agreed to increase tobacco taxes by $2.00 per pack after defeating a similar proposal in 2012.

The public doesn't always agree to increases, however. The voters soundly rejected a 2006 initiative that would have added an additional tax bracket of 1.7 percent beyond the highest level for individuals with taxable incomes of $400,000 or more, with the revenues earmarked for a statewide preschool program. In 2009, Governor Schwarzenegger and the legislature strung together five ballot proposals that would simultaneously cap spending and temporarily increase sales taxes (0.25 percent), income taxes (1 percent), and motor vehicle fees (0.50 percent). The public refused all five propositions.

Perhaps the most dramatic tax-altering event came in 1978 with the passage of **Proposition 13**, an initiative that reduced local property taxes by 57 percent. Since then, property owners have saved more than $528 billion in taxes,[3] while local governments have leaned on the state for relief. As a result, the state has become the major funder for local services such as public education, although support has varied with the health of the economy. This uncertainty has brought endless criticism from local government officials.

The bottom line is that there are many more players in the budget process than meet the eye. This complexity both slows down the process and requires near unanimity among the various parties before any major decisions are made.

REVENUE SOURCES

Like most states, California relies on several forms of taxation for its general fund budget (that is, the budget exclusive of federal funds). The largest sources of revenue are personal income tax, sales tax, and corporation taxes. Smaller revenue supplies come from motor vehicle fees as well as fuel, insurance, tobacco, and alcohol taxes. The state's major revenue sources and expenditures for fiscal year 2016–2017 are shown in Figure 8.1.

Other taxes are levied by local governments. (See Chapter 9.) Chief among these is the property tax, although its use was reduced considerably by Proposition 13. This tax is collected by counties rather than by the state, but the state

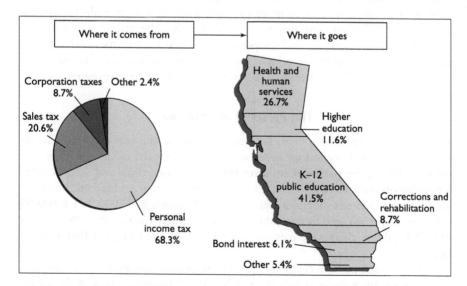

FIGURE 8.1   California's Revenue Sources and Expenditures, 2014–2016.
SOURCE: Governor's Office.

allocates it among the different levels of local government, and it still is a part—directly or indirectly—of the tax burden of all Californians.

Because public opinion polls generally reveal an anti-tax mood among the voters, policy makers have refused to add taxes to cope with burgeoning needs. Instead, they hand new tax decisions to the voters in the form of occasional state ballot initiatives. As a result, the state's commitments to most services have decreased considerably over the past three decades. Individual recipients, school districts, and local governments have been thrown into turmoil. Infrastructure projects, such as highway maintenance programs and Sacramento delta levee repairs, have been stretched out. A 2016 study found that the state had deferred maintenance obligations of $77 billion on transportation systems, water facilities, and other government services, yet the budget allocated $500 million for the fiscal year.[4] Absent major revenue-creating decisions, there is little chance of closing the gap in the near future.

The Sales Tax

Until the Great Depression of 1929, a relatively small state government garnered funds by relying on minor taxes on businesses and utilities. After the economic crash, however, the state was forced to develop new tax sources to cope with hard times. The **sales tax**, a levy of 2.5 percent on certain goods and products except food, was adopted to provide permanent funding for schools and local governments.

Today, the statewide sales tax base is 7.25 percent. (An additional 0.25 tacked on courtesy of Proposition 30 expired on December 31, 2016.) Of that amount, cities and counties get 2 percent to help meet health and public safety needs. In addition, when the legislature passed Governor Brown's prison realignment plan in 2015, 1.06 percent of the state portion was set aside for county management of transferred prisoners to local jails. The state keeps the rest. Beyond the base, as much as 2.25 percent is tacked on by cities and counties for various needs, most of which are transportation related. The sales tax accounts for about 20.6 percent of the state's general fund tax revenues.

The Personal Income Tax

A second major revenue source, the personal income tax, was modeled after its federal counterpart to collect greater amounts of money from residents with greater earnings. Today, the **personal income tax** varies between 1.0 and 12.3 percent, depending on one's income. The 11.3 percent and 12.3 percent brackets, however, are temporary additions for individuals earning between $350,000 and $500,000 and more than $500,000. First scheduled to expire in 2018 as a result of Proposition 30 in 2012, the surcharges were extended to 2030 with the passage of **Proposition 55** in 2016.

The personal income tax is now the fastest growing component of state revenue (see Figure 8.2)—a significant fact because Californians ranked thirteenth among the fifty states in per capita income in 2014. These days, the personal

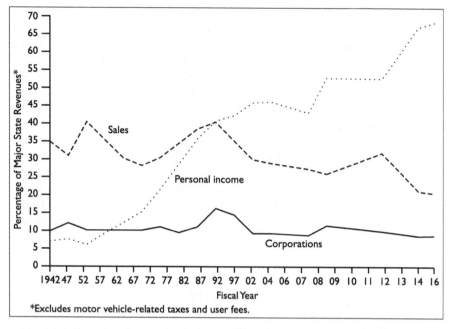

FIGURE 8.2 California's Tax Burden, 1942–2016.
SOURCE: Department of Finance.

income tax accounts for 68.3 percent of the state tax bite, leaving some observers to wonder whether the state is overly dependent on one revenue source.

Corporation Taxes

Corporation income taxes contribute much less to California's budget than do sales and personal income taxes. Since 1996, the corporate tax rate has remained at 8.84 percent. Corporation taxes now account for about 8.7 percent of state revenues. Corporate taxes comprised nearly 16 percent of the state's general fund revenues as recently as 1978, but several rate reductions and tax exemptions created by the legislature have reduced the burden considerably.

Aside from Proposition 13 and the reliance on **user taxes**, such as those levied on gasoline and cigarettes, California's revenue collection system has undergone gradual adjustments over the past sixty years. Figure 8.2 shows the changing weight of the sales, personal income, and corporation taxes from 1942 to the present. Along with a steady drift toward increased dependence on the personal income tax, the state has experienced decreased dependence on sales and corporation taxes.

Taxes in Perspective

Viewed in a comparative context, the overall tax burden for California ranks eighth in the nation on a per capita basis. Nevertheless, there have been changes in the state tax blend, with the state becoming increasingly dependent on the personal income tax as its primary source of income.

In terms of categories, the state ranks first in personal income taxes, eighth in corporation taxes, tenth in sales taxes, and thirty-fourth in property taxes.[5] In other revenue areas, California taxes are near the bottom. For example, the state ranks forty-ninth in both fuel taxes and alcoholic beverage taxes. With respect to tobacco taxes, California ranked thirty-fifth in the nation[6] until 2016, when the voters passed Proposition 56, which added $2.00 to the tobacco tax. The state now ranks ninth. With respect to an oil severance tax, California is the only one of fourteen major oil-producing states that does not tax oil.

Some of this is due to the influence of powerful interest groups, but much of the problem stems from the state's dramatic shift to a service economy, where no services are subject to the sales tax. The result is a system that is overly dependent upon the personal income tax, the collections from which can swing greatly with the state of the economy.

SPENDING

The annual state budget addresses thousands of financial commitments, both large and small. Public education (grades K–12) receives the most support, followed by health and welfare, higher education, and prisons. Outlays in these four areas account for more than 90 percent of the general fund. The remainder of the budget goes to designated long-term projects such as transportation, parks, and veterans' programs, many of which have been authorized by public ballot or include federal funds.

Since 1979, several voter-passed ballot propositions have created a budget system that is largely formula-driven. K–12 public education, transportation programs, and mental health are among the many program areas for which either percentages of the budget or specific revenues are directed for specific areas. Thus, public education receives at least 40 percent of the general fund unless two-thirds of the legislature grants a waiver because of a fiscal emergency. Likewise, motor vehicle fees are directed exclusively for transportation-related services and projects. Some critics have characterized the formula approach as a political "straitjacket" that is unresponsive to changing times and needs. Defenders of "formula government" argue that it is the only way to keep state leaders from operating with a blank check.

Public Education: Grades K through 12

The state constitution gives public education a "superior right" to state funds; as such, public schools get the largest share of the state budget. Local school districts periodically add relatively small amounts to education through voter-approved bonds and parcel taxes, but the preponderance of support comes from the state legislature through its annual allocations.

Funding for public education in California has an uneven history. The state ranked among the top-funded states throughout the 1950s and 1960s, thanks to abundant revenue streams from state and local government sources. Then the pattern changed. Passage of Proposition 13 in 1978 reduced property taxes by 57 percent, slashing the ability of local governments to fund public education. Local governments depended upon the state to make up the difference, but policy makers were caught between too many priorities and inadequate resources. In 1988, the state committed 37 percent of the general fund to K–12 public education. That same year, amid growing concerns about weak funding and poor classroom performance, education reformers secured voter approval of **Proposition 98**, a measure that established 40 percent as a minimum state budget funding threshold except in times of fiscal emergency. With this mandate, the state poured money into reducing class sizes in grades K through 3 and lengthened the school year from 180 to 190 days. But the upward direction was short-lived.

State aid for public education has dropped precipitously with declining state revenues. Between 2008 and 2014 alone, support fell from $50.3 billion to $45.0 billion. Only in 2016 did the state surpass its commitment from 2008. At $11,145 per student (2014–2015 figures), California expenditures remain nearly $600 below the national average,[7] and thousands more below comparable industrialized states. The school year minimum has fallen to 175 days, three full weeks less classroom instruction than twenty years ago. Only four states require less attendance from their students. California ranks fiftieth among the states in its student–teacher ratio, a commonly used criterion for assessing education effectiveness. Although the home of high tech, the state is one of thirteen states to receive an F grade from the U.S. Chamber of Commerce in classroom technology instruction.[8]

All this has produced a sorry, if not unexpected, outcome in terms of high school graduation, where the state ranks tied with two other states for thirtieth. According to the National Assessment of Educational Progress, a well-known nonprofit group, California hovers near the bottom of almost every assessment category. Table 8.1 shows the most recent data available. Nevertheless, California has made modest improvements in closing the gap and now ranks 21 in per capita spending for K–12 public education. More funds may be forthcoming with the allocation of Proposition 30 and extension of those funds through **Proposition 55**, although a slowing economy may keep the state from moving ahead. Still, there is much work to be done.

T A B L E 8.1 California Rankings in Key Education Categories

Category	Rank	Year
Reading, 4th grade	49	2014
Reading, 8th grade	44	2014
Math, 4th grade	48	2014
Math, 8th grade	41	2014
Science, 8th grade	48 (tied)	2014

SOURCE: National Assessment of Education Progress, 2015.

With Latino and Asian American students accounting for 54 percent and 9 percent of the school population, respectively, language-related issues have emerged. In 1994 the passage of **Proposition 227**, a measure limiting bilingual education for non-English-speaking students to one year, added to the debate over how to "mainstream" the diverse California student community. In 2016, the voters passed **Proposition 58**, which removed the bilingual limitations imposed by Proposition 227. All of this has occurred in a state where 22 percent of all public school students are "English learners" (English is not the first language), compared with 9 percent nationally.

There are chilling consequences from these policies. For starters, there are wide variations with respect to those who do graduate. While 87 percent of non-Hispanic whites graduated in 2014, the rates for Latinos and African Americans were 76 percent and 68 percent, respectively. Meanwhile, Asian Americans had the most success with a rate of 92 percent.[9] Many of those who do graduate high school are unprepared for college. A California State University study found that more than one-third of the incoming freshman class needed remedial instruction in English, math, or both.[10] Combined with the state's poor student performance on national tests, neither of these statistics points to educational excellence.

Nevertheless, the debate goes on. Some reformers have turned to "charter schools"—independent, community-controlled alternatives to what many describe as a broken system. As of 2015, there were about 1,200 charter schools in California, still a small number compared with the state's 10,400 traditional public schools, although double the number in 2008. Thus far, there is no consensus that the education products of those schools exceed those of traditional public schools.

The process of fixing California's K–12 public education problems will be neither quick nor cheap. In 2007 a 1,700-page report commissioned by Governor Arnold Schwarzenegger declared that it would cost a staggering $1.5 trillion more each year to make all students academically proficient in traditional core knowledge areas such as reading, math, and science. In 2013, Governor Jerry Brown proposed and the state legislature passed the **Local Control Funding Formula**, a program that dedicates more than $2 billion annually to schools with English learners and poor students. The idea is to direct additional resources to those who need help the most. The Local Control Funding Formula is a beginning, but it would seem that even more resources will be needed to address California's K–12 education deficiencies.

Higher Education: Colleges and Universities

California's budget woes have cut deeply into support for higher education. Once viewed as the role model for public universities, the higher education system has suffered from a lack of funding and greatly reduced admission slots.

Three units share responsibility for higher education in the state. The state's 113 two-year community colleges enroll about 2.1 million students. Historically, community colleges have been the entry-level institutions for students who otherwise did not qualify for, or who could not afford to attend, California's four-year public universities. They also provide valuable training programs. Funding for community colleges is connected to the formula for primary and secondary public schools, courtesy of Proposition 98. Between 2008 and 2012, state revenue losses from the Great Recession led to a 13 percent drop in support, resulting in 21 percent fewer classes and 500,000 fewer students. Meanwhile, student fees increased to $36 per unit from $26 per unit. Since then, the state has increased support by 23 percent, thanks largely to the passage of Proposition 30 and to economic recovery. During the same period, funding has increased by 31 percent.[11]

California community colleges provide more than one-fourth of the students attending the University of California (UC) and about half of those enrolled in the California State University (CSU) systems. With 238,000 students, UC educates both undergraduate and graduate students at ten campuses throughout the state. Designated as the state's primary research university, UC awards almost all professional degrees (such as medical and law degrees) and doctorates in the public higher education system. The California State University (CSU) system, with 474,000 students at twenty-three campuses, concentrates on undergraduate instruction, most commonly awarding master's degrees in such fields as education, engineering, and business.

State support for public universities was fairly constant until the 1990s, holding at about 11 percent of the general fund budget, and peaking at 12.7 percent during the 2002–2003 fiscal year. For fiscal year 2016–2017, 11.6 percent of the general fund was dedicated to the public universities. But the state's share of the cost of education has decreased dramatically. For example, whereas the state general fund provided 90 percent of UC's education costs in 1969–1970, support dropped to 9 percent by 2016–2017. And at CSU, the 90 percent paid by the state in 1969–1970 fell to 56 percent by 2016–2017.

Students have been forced to make up the shortfall. At both UC and CSU, student fees have more than tripled between 2003–2004 and 2016–2017. Meanwhile, lacking state budget support and with much higher tuition, the state's universities have looked to non-Californians and significantly higher out-of-state tuition prices to help make up budget deficits. Between 2010 and 2014, the number of California residents attending actually declined by 1 percent, while students from out-of-state increased by 82 percent, much to the dismay of qualified in-state residents.[12] The new emphasis may have caused difficulties for in-state applicants, but the presence of non-residents has brought $400 million in badly needed revenues to UC. In 2015, out-of-state students paid $37,000 in tuition for the year, whereas in-state student residents paid $12,400. In 2016, after considerable public anger and the threat of legislative oversight, UC increased its in-state admissions.[13] But as long as funding woes continue, the issue of in-state versus out-of-state admissions is unlikely to go away.

Health and Human Services

Health and human services programs receive the second-largest share of the state budget, amounting for more than one-fourth of general fund outlays.

The programs accounting for the most significant state commitment include California Work Opportunity and Responsibility to Kids (CalWORKs), Medi-Cal, and the Supplemental Security Income (SSI) program. Medi-Cal provides health care benefits for the poor, and SSI offers state assistance to the elderly and the disabled. But no program is as politically charged as CalWORKs, the primary welfare program.

California has sizable welfare costs. With about 12.5 percent of the nation's population, the state is home to 25 percent of all welfare recipients. This is due, in part, to the fact that California has the highest poverty rate in the nation, something that people overlook given the state's great wealth. The numbers have been growing. In 1990, California had 10.5 percent of the nation's population and 12 percent of all welfare recipients.

As welfare numbers have increased, per capita government spending for programs has gone down. Changes in state policy began in 1997 after Congress passed the Welfare Reform Act, limiting welfare payments to no more than five years. Shortly thereafter, the legislature passed its CalWORKs legislation, which provides cash grants and welfare-to-work services for needy families with children ten years of age or younger and requires all adults to work at least thirty-two hours per week. The eligibility period was reduced to four years under the Schwarzenegger administration.

As of 2016, about 1.1 million California children were CalWORKs recipients, representing about 565,000 families. The cost was $5.5 billion, with the federal government picking up 60 percent of the tab. In fiscal year 2016–2017, the maximum monthly welfare payment for a family of four (one parent and three children) was $840.

Prisons

Of the major state allocation categories, the budgets for prisons and corrections have grown the most in recent years. As with education, the public has played a role in this policy area. Several initiatives have established mandatory prison terms for various crimes and extended the terms for many other crimes. The most sweeping changes occurred in 1994, when the legislature (and later the voters, through an initiative) enacted a new **three strikes** law for repeat felons. As of 2012, about 9,000 of the state's 130,000 prisoners were incarcerated under the three-strikes classification.

Because of the three-strikes law and other policy changes, California's prison population swelled beyond belief. In 1994, the total prison population was 125,000. It jumped to 168,000 by 2009, with the cost for incarceration averaging $49,000 per convict per year. The demographics of the prison population also have changed: 42 percent Latino, 29 percent African American, 6 percent others, and 27 percent white, as of 2015. Phenomenal incarceration growth has forced the construction of new prisons.

Between 1994 and 2012, corrections and rehabilitation comprised the fastest growing area of state spending, ultimately reaching 10 percent of the annual budget. But prisoner lawsuits on overcrowding and medical conditions resulted in the federal courts ordering the state to reduce the number of inmates by at least 45,000 inmates to better match the prison population with prison capacity. Governor Jerry Brown responded to the order by creating a program to move 30,000 of the state's least violent offenders to county jails with the promise of state funds to accompany the shift. Under his plan known as **realignment**, sentencing and parole protocols were altered to permit more inmates either in county jails or out under local supervision. Also in 2012, the voters passed **Proposition 36**, which made it easier for about 3,000 nonviolent offenders to request reduced sentences.

The new policy enabled the state to reduce state spending on incarceration to 8.7 percent of the state budget by 2016–2017. Yet, other problems have developed. Although the state committed to covering the local government costs associated with realignment, local officials complained that they were not fully compensated; many also grumbled that the overcrowding problem had simply shifted from the state to local level.[14]

Other Budget Obligations

Managing California's budget is a difficult task even in the best of economic times. During the Great Recession, the state suffered huge deficits and plunged into debt from which it has only recently recovered. On the expenditure side of the budget ledger, out-of-control prison spending and welfare costs have leveled off, and in the case of prisons, costs have actually gone down. Public education expenditures, however, still leave California below the national average, despite recent voter-approved initiatives. Two other less known, yet fast-growing, state expenditure categories are payment of bond debt and pension payouts. Together, they now consume close to 10 percent of the state general fund and show little sign of slowing down.

Bonds.   While voter-approved borrowing through bonds represents an "easy" way to fund major projects over time, cumulatively these bonds are taking a toll on the state. California now ranks tenth among the states in per capita bond debt, up from thirty-second in 1991. Our propensity to rely upon bonds has reduced the state's credit rating, which adds to the interest costs of bonds. In 2015–2016, interest on bonds was about 6.1 percent of the state budget, or $7.5 billion. That's a substantial commitment, but down considerably from 2012–2013, when the state paid $8.6 billion in interest, or 8.8 percent of the budget. To the extent that the state is able to reduce reliance on bonds, California will have more money available for various services and programs.[15]

Retirement Pensions.   California's massive public employee pension program, the California Public Employees' Retirement System (CalPERS), covers more than 1.7 million employees, retirees, and their families, or about 4.3 percent of the state's population. Just over 560,000 are retirees who have worked for various state government agencies or their survivors. Employees contribute a small portion of their salary to the program, with the state providing the rest as part of the salary compensation package. For years, CalPERS gushed with surpluses, thanks to a robust financial market that contained most of the fund's investments. Since the onslaught of the recession in 2008, CalPERS payments have exceeded revenues. By law, the state must make up for any shortfall, and that money comes out of the state budget. In fiscal year 2016–2017, the state was required pay out $5.4 billion of the general fund into CalPERS—five times the amount paid a decade earlier. Because of spiraling costs, Governor Jerry Brown and the legislature enacted new cost control legislation in 2012, requiring higher employee contributions and extending retirement ages. Additional pension reform measures are likely to be considered in the coming years.

CALIFORNIA'S BUDGET: TOO LITTLE, TOO MUCH, OR JUST RIGHT?

Have you ever met anyone who claims that he or she should pay more taxes? Neither have we. Almost everybody dislikes paying taxes, and almost everybody thinks that the money collected is spent incorrectly or unwisely. That seems to be a perennial dilemma in California. However, although most people oppose increased taxes, they also oppose program cuts. It's a modern-day dilemma for state policy makers and the public alike.

Like their counterparts elsewhere, California policy makers have struggled to find a fair system of taxation to pay for needed programs. Given the involvement of so many public and private interests, however, it's difficult to determine what is fair. Moreover, during the past few decades, taxation and budget decisions have been subject to radical change. Somehow, the state's infrastructure has survived, although critics have been less than thrilled with the fiscal uncertainty that has become commonplace in California government.

NOTES

1. "Key Facts about California Surface Transportation System and Federal Funding," TRIP, Washington, DC, January 2016, www.tripnet.org/docs/Fact_Sheet_CA.pdf.

2. "Just the Facts: Californians and Transportation," Public Policy Institute of California, June 2016, p. 1, www.ppic.org/main/publication_show.asp?i=1204.

3. Howard Jarvis Taxpayers Association, 2009, www.hjta.org/index.php.

4. "The 2016-17 Budget: Governor's General Fund Deferred Maintenance Proposal," Legislative Analyst's Office, Sacramento, CA, February 2016, p. 1.

5. "State Taxes," Tax Foundation, Washington, DC, February 2016, http://tax foundation.org/tax-topics/state-taxes; and "How High Are the Property Taxes in Your State," Tax Foundation, Washington, DC, August 13, 2015, http://tax foundation.org/blog/how-high-are-property-taxes-your-state.

6. "State Cigarette Excise Taxes Rankings and Ratings," Campaign for Tobacco-Free Kids, Washington, DC, July 6, 2016, www.tobaccofreekids.org/research/factsheets/pdf/0097.pdf.

7. "Rankings of the States 2015 and Estimates of School Statistics 2016," National Education Association, Washington, DC, May 2016, p. 55.

8. "Leaders and Laggards: A State-by-State Report Card on K-12 Educational Effectiveness," U.S. Chamber of Commerce, Washington, DC, 2014, p. 35.

9. "State Schools Chief Tom Torlakson Reports Record High Graduation Rate," California Department of Education, Sacramento, CA, April 29, 2015.

10. "More than a Third of Cal State Freshmen Ill-Prepared for College-Level Math, English," KPPC Radio, February 19, 2014, www.scpr.org/blogs/education/2014/02/19/15882/more-than-a-third-of-cal-state-freshman-ill-prepar.

11. See "Higher Education Analysis: The 2016-2017 Budget," Legislative Analyst's Office, Sacramento, CA, February 28, 2016, www.lao.ca.gov/Publications/Report/3372; and "The 2015-2016 Budget: California Community Colleges," Legislative Analyst's Office, April 8, 2015, www.lao.ca.gov/handouts/education/2015/2015-16-budget-CCC-040815.pdf.

12. "UC Seeks Out-of-State Students, Tuition," *San Francisco Chronicle*, July 10, 2016, p. C1.

13. "After Outcry, University of California Increases In-State Admission Offers," *New York Times*, July 12, 2016, www.nytimes.com/2016/07/13/us/after-outcry-university-of-california-increases-in-state-admission-offers.html?_r=0.

14. "Gov. Jerry Brown's Prison Reforms Haven't Lived Up to His Billing," *Los Angeles Times*, June 21, 2014, www.latimes.com/local/politics/la-me-ff-pol-brown-prisons-20140622-story.html#page=1.

15. "Debt Affordability Report," Office of the State Treasurer, Sacramento, CA, October 2013, p. 11.

LEARN MORE ON THE WEB

California Budget Project:
www.cbp.org

California state budget—Department of Finance:
www.dof.ca.gov

California state budget—Legislature:
www.lao.ca.gov

California Taxpayers' Association:

www.caltax.org

California Tax Reform Association:
www.caltaxreform.org

National Center for Education Statistics:
www.nces.ed.gov

National Governors Association:
www.nga.org

GET INVOLVED

Track a state budget item such as K–12 funding, prisons, or another policy area over the past decade. Has it increased or decreased more than you imagined? Should there be more of less spending? If more, what would you rely upon for funding? If less, what would you do with the leftover funds?

9

California's Local Governments: Politics at the Grassroots

LEARNING OBJECTIVES

9.1 Compare and contrast the functions and structures of cities and counties.

9.2 Identify local governments in addition to cities and counties.

9.3 Describe the sources of revenues for cities and counties.

9.4 Discuss the fiscal problems and constraints of local governments.

What's the point of having local governments as well as state government, and why so many, anyway?

The actions of state and national governments get lots of news coverage and are important, but what local governments do often has a greater impact on our daily lives than the more distant state government. City governments make decisions about the traffic on our streets; safety in our neighborhoods; and access to parks, libraries, and affordable housing. County governments manage transit systems and provide health care and social services to those most in need, including people who are homeless, mentally ill, or impoverished. School districts educate our children—sometimes well and sometimes not so well.

State governments delegate these functions to local entities because they can be accomplished better by a local rather than statewide agency or because communities have demanded local control or even because the state just doesn't want to perform the service. These local entities are either directly created by the states or by citizens through a process structured by the states. The rights and duties of local governments are assigned by the states, mandating some responsibilities and prohibiting others. States also allocate taxing powers and may share revenues with local governments. States retain the ultimate authority, however, so they can change the rights and powers granted to local governments, expanding or reducing their tasks, funding, and independence. Local leaders complain when states tell them to do things they don't think they can afford or take away previously committed funds to balance the state budget.

The power of the state notwithstanding, local government is often where democracy works best, simply because it's closer to us than Sacramento or Washington, D.C. We can participate directly in local politics precisely because it's local. We can volunteer for candidates, whom we can actually meet and get to know; we can even run for office ourselves. We can lobby elected officials without relying on paid professionals. We can attend city council meetings and testify in person. We can find allies and form interest groups like those described in Chapter 4 (and all those types exist in communities). Millions of people participate constantly in local politics—go to your own city hall and see for yourself.

COUNTIES AND CITIES

Cities and counties are the primary local governments in California as in other states. Our 58 counties and 482 cities were created in slightly different ways and perform distinctly different tasks.[1]

Counties

California is divided into counties (see the map inside the front cover) ranging in size from San Francisco's 47 square miles to San Bernardino County's 20,164, and ranging in population from Alpine County's 1,110 residents to Los Angeles County's 10,170,298. **Counties** function both as local governments and as administrative units of the state. As local governments, counties provide police and fire protection, maintain roads, and perform other services for rural and **unincorporated areas** (those that are not part of any city). They also run jails; operate transit systems; protect health and sanitation; and keep records on property, marriages, and deaths. As agencies of the state, counties oversee elections, operate the courts, administer the state's welfare system, and collect some taxes. The responsibilities of counties were expanded in 2012, when the **realignment** program of Governor **Jerry Brown** moved the incarceration of nonviolent felons from state prisons to county jails, where costs are much lower. Even after reimbursing the cost to counties, the state saved millions of dollars. Some counties complained, however, that their reimbursements don't cover the costs imposed on them by realignment.

State law prescribes the organization of county government. The governing body for counties is a five-member **board of supervisors** elected by district to staggered four-year terms. Supervisors' salaries range from around $25,000 a year in Alpine County to $285,388 in Los Angeles County. The board sets county policies; oversees the budget; and hires a chief administrator, or **county executive**, to carry out its programs. County executives are usually paid two or three times as much as their bosses, the elected supervisors. In addition to the board of supervisors, voters elect the sheriff, district attorney, tax assessor, and sometimes other department heads (see Figure 9.1). Like county supervisors, these officials serve

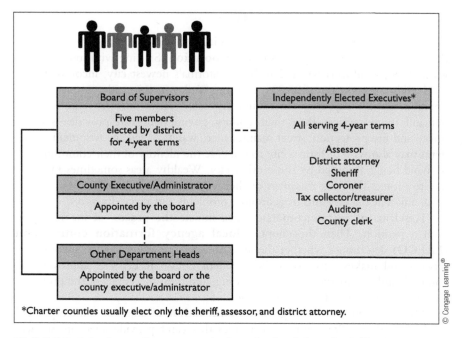

FIGURE 9.1 County Government: An Organizational Chart for California's Forty-Four General Law Counties.

four-year terms and are chosen in **nonpartisan** elections, a Progressive legacy that keeps party labels off the ballot. As of 2016, 83 percent of California's 296 elected county supervisors are white, and 77 percent are male.

Although most counties operate with these state-dictated structures (known as a **general-law** system because it applies to multiple counties), the state also gives counties the option to organize their own structures by drafting their own **charters**. Fourteen counties have done so, including Los Angeles, Sacramento, San Diego, and Santa Clara. County voters must approve the charter and any proposed amendments. Generally, a "home rule" or **charter county** uses its local option to replace elected executives with appointees of the board of supervisors or to strengthen the powers of the appointed county executive.

San Francisco, uniquely among California's local governments, operates as both a city and a county. Most counties have several cities within their boundaries, but the separate city and county governments of San Francisco were consolidated in 1911. San Francisco thus has a board of supervisors with eleven members rather than a city council, but unlike any other county, it also has a mayor.

No new county has been formed in California since 1907, although in some large counties such as Los Angeles, San Bernardino, and Santa Barbara, rural areas frustrated by urban domination have tried unsuccessfully to break away and form their own jurisdictions.

Cities

While counties are created by the state, **cities** are established at the request of their citizens through the process of **incorporation**. Starting with just eight cities in 1850, California has 482 today. California's newest city, incorporated in 2011 with a population of 98,030, is Jurupa Valley in Riverside County. Incorporation usually happens when unincorporated areas urbanize and residents demand more services than their county government can provide—such as police and fire protection, street maintenance, water, or sewage treatment. Residents may also wish to form a city to preserve the identity of their community or to avoid being absorbed by some other city. Wealthy areas sometimes incorporate to protect their tax resources or their ethnic homogeneity from the impact of an adjacent big city and its economic problems and racial diversity.

Residents of an unincorporated area initiate the process of incorporation with a petition. Then the county's **local agency formation commission (LAFCO)** determines whether the area has a sufficient tax base to support city services and makes sense as an independent entity. If LAFCO approves, the county board of supervisors holds a hearing, and then the voters of the proposed city approve or reject the incorporation.

Once formed, cities can grow by **annexation** of adjacent unincorporated (county) territory. Sometimes, small cities that can't provide adequate services disband themselves by consolidating with an adjacent city. More rarely, people in an existing city seek to de-annex, or secede. The 1.7 million residents of the San Fernando Valley and other parts of the city of Los Angeles who felt ignored by their city government attempted to secede in 2002, but voters in the city as a whole, who must agree to any secession, rejected the plan.

Like California counties, most California cities operate under state law, which prescribes their governmental structures. Referred to as **general law cities**, they typically have a five-member **city council**, with members elected in nonpartisan elections for four-year terms. The council appoints a **city manager** to supervise daily operations; the manager, in turn, appoints department heads such as the police and fire chiefs (see Figure 9.2). Most council members as well as mayors and county supervisors are not restricted by **term limits**, but several counties and over forty cities limit elected officials to two or sometimes three four-year terms.

Cities with populations exceeding 3,500 may choose to write their own charters. A hundred and twenty-one California cities have done so. A **charter city** has more discretion in choosing the structure of its government than a general law city does, as well as somewhat greater fiscal flexibility and policy-making authority, provided that no state law supersedes their actions. California's largest cities all have their own charters.

Even when a city is incorporated, the county provides for courts, jails, social services, elections, tax collection, public health, and public transit, but once incorporated, a city takes on extensive responsibilities, including police and fire protection, sewage treatment, garbage disposal, parks and recreational services, libraries, streets and traffic management, and land use planning. The latter is

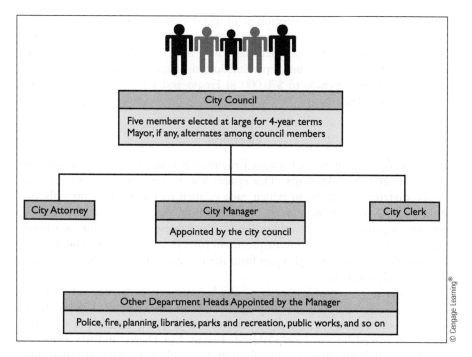

FIGURE 9.2 City Government: An Organizational Chart for California's 361 General Law Cities.

arguably the greatest power given to cities. By zoning land for particular uses—housing, offices, shopping centers, or industry—city governments determine the nature of their communities as well as their financial resources, since some land uses generate more tax revenue than others.

POWER IN THE CITY: COUNCIL MEMBERS, MANAGERS, AND MAYORS

Most of California's cities have five-member councils with appointed city managers as executives, as set forth by state law. Some larger and older cities have developed municipal government structures uniquely suited to their own needs and preferences. For example, the role and powers of executives vary among California cities; some opt for a stronger mayor rather than the manager prescribed by the state for general law cities. Similarly, city councils may be chosen in different ways or expanded in size to allow for more representation. Los Angeles has fifteen council members, San Jose ten, and San Diego eight. San Francisco's board of supervisors numbers eleven. City council members and mayors in most cities are paid only a token salary because they're not expected to be full-time employees. Many, however, are devoted public servants who spend well over forty hours a week at their work—for paltry pay. The annual salary for a Rancho Cucamonga city council member, like those of most other small cities, is $15,716. Larger cities pay more with the expectation of full-time representation, although compensation varies from $41,376 a year in Riverside to $70,000 in Fresno and a high of $184,610 in the City of Los Angeles.

Elections

In most California cities, each council member is chosen by voters throughout the city in **at-large elections**. This system was created by the Progressives to replace **district elections**, in which each council member represents only part of the city. At-large elections were intended to reduce the parochial influence of machine-organized ethnic neighborhoods. The strategy worked, but as a result, even when minority groups are majorities in parts of a city, their candidates have been unable to secure enough votes from the city as a whole to win at large, and so were rarely elected.

As cities grew, citywide campaigns also became extremely costly. To increase minority representation and cut campaign costs, some cities have returned to district elections. Los Angeles has used district elections since 1924; Sacramento converted in 1971, followed by San Jose, Oakland, Fresno, San Diego, and San Francisco. Over forty California cities use some form of district elections. Most are large cities, and most have reverted to district elections through voter-approved charter amendments. Others such as Merced (2016) switched in response to lawsuits from minority residents arguing that their at-large elections systematically discriminated against minority candidates. Several other cities with white councils but majority-minority populations is made up of minorities face similar lawsuits.

Where they are in use, district elections have increased opportunities for minority candidates, but overall, minorities remain substantially underrepresented among California's local elected officials. Women and minority candidates, as well as gay and lesbian candidates, have been more successful in local elections than in state elections, but they are still held back by discrimination, low participation, at-large elections, and the cost of campaigns.

In most California cities, council members are chosen in single elections; the candidate who gets the most votes wins, even if he or she doesn't get a majority. In larger cities and in cities that elect their council members by district, if no candidate wins a majority in the primary election, the top two compete in a **runoff election**, ensuring that the winner is elected with a majority. Critics have objected to the high cost of such elections—both to taxpayers and in campaign spending. In 2004, San Francisco addressed these concerns with **ranked-choice voting**, in which voters rank their top three choices of candidates in order of preference. Oakland and Berkeley followed with the same system in 2010. If no candidate wins a majority, the candidate with the fewest votes is eliminated and those votes are assigned to the voters' second choice—and so on until one candidate attains a majority. In the 2010 mayoral election in Oakland, the candidate who came in second won the election when the second and third choice votes were counted—much to the chagrin of some voters (she lost her bid for reelection in 2014). Supporters of this system claim that it saves time and money, but voters and candidates found its implementation confusing.

Whatever the system, voter participation varies greatly among cities. Voter participation or turnout is generally higher in cities with elected mayors and district elections, but the key factor related to turnout is when the elections are held. About one-third of California's cities hold their elections separately from state and national elections. Median turnout in these elections is less than 30 percent.[2] Los Angeles, for example, holds its elections separately, and turnout in that city's 2015 election was 10 percent. Lower turnout affects outcomes because the composition of the electorate changes along with the number of voters; older, more affluent voters predominate, giving an advantage to more conservative candidates. Researchers report that in cities with low voter turnout, less money is spent on programs that might help the poor and more goes to downtown development and other projects that aid business. In short, local governments spend their revenues on those who vote.[3]

Turnout in cities that hold elections concurrently with state and national elections is nearly twice as high as in cities with separate elections.[4] Concern about low turnout in separate or **isolated elections** resulted in a 2013 charter amendment in Los Angeles, where local elections will be held concurrently with state elections beginning in 2020. A new state law prohibiting separate elections where voter participation is 25 percent less than the average turnout in a local entity in previous statewide elections is likely to shake up politics in other communities that currently use isolated elections. This could affect many cities, school districts, and special districts, but all elections in California counties are already held at the same time as the state and national elections. Voting for local officials may still be lower, however, due to "drop-off," with some voters declining to cast ballots because of lack of interest or information.

As with state-level campaigns, local reformers have been concerned about the costs of city and county races and the influence of money on politics. Spending on local campaigns has risen steadily since the 1980s, when professional campaign consultants and their techniques (see Chapter 3) became common in local races. About one-third of California's cities and counties have enacted local campaign-finance laws, requiring disclosure of contributors and expenditures and sometimes limiting contributions. Los Angeles and a few other cities restrict spending and provide limited public financing for campaigns. Even in these communities, however, independent political action committees raise and spend substantial sums on campaigns separately from the candidates.

Executive Power

Most people assume that **mayors** lead cities and have substantial power, but that's not usually the case in California communities. Because mayors were once connected with political machines, the Progressive reformers shifted executive authority to council-appointed city managers who were intended to be neutral, professional administrators. Most California cities use this **council–manager**

system. While the manager administers the city's programs, appoints department heads, and proposes the budget, the council members alternate as mayor—a ceremonial post that involves chairing meetings and cutting ribbons.

San Francisco, however, uses a **strong-mayor form of government**, in which the mayor is elected directly by the people to a four-year term and holds powers similar to those of the president in the national system, including the veto, budget control, and appointment of department heads. Voters in Los Angeles gave their mayor enhanced authority, including the power to appoint forty-four department heads, when they approved a new charter in 1999. Fresno (in 1997), Oakland (in 1998), and San Diego (in 2005) have also switched to a strong-mayor form of government.

Other cities in California have also moved away from the pure council–manager system of government. While retaining their city managers, one-third of California cities have revised the system so that the mayor is directly elected and serves a four-year term. Some have also increased the powers of their mayors, although they continue to sit and vote as council members. Even without much authority, being a directly elected mayor brings visibility and influence. Mayors of Long Beach and San Jose, for example, exert substantial clout despite their limited official power.

The salaries of city executives vary greatly. Mayors of smaller cities exercise little authority and are paid only token wages, like council members in those cities. The mayor of Bakersfield, for example, is paid $24,000 a year. Mayors with greater authority are paid more, ranging from $100,464 in San Diego to $232,426 in Los Angeles. City managers, however, are universally paid more than elected officials, averaging around $200,000 per year—less in smaller cities and more in larger ones.

Looking to the future, the balance of power between managers as professional administrators and mayors as political leaders will probably continue to shift in favor of stronger mayors, partly because of media attention but also because of the need for political leadership in the tempest of city politics. Elected officials and community groups often complain about the inherent lack of direct accountability in the city manager form of government, in which the executive, who never has to face election, is insulated from the voters. Giving more authority to mayors and council members makes accountability more direct, but it may also decrease the professionalism of local government.

MORE GOVERNMENTS

In addition to cities and counties, California has thousands of other, less visible local governments (see Table 9.1). Created by the state or by citizens, they provide designated services and have taxing powers, mostly by collecting small portions of property taxes paid by homeowners and businesses or by charging for their services. Yet except for school districts, most of us are unaware of their existence.

T A B L E 9.1 California's Local Governments, 2015

Type	Number
Counties	58
Cities	482
School Districts	1,022
Special Districts	5,141
TOTAL	6,703

SOURCE: California State Controller, www.sco.ca.gov; and Ed-Data, www.ed-data.com.

School Districts and Special Districts

In California, K–12 education is provided by 1,022 **school districts**. They are created and overseen by the state and governed by elected boards, which appoint professional educators as superintendents to oversee day-to-day operations. Except for parents and teachers, whose involvement is intense, voter participation in school elections and politics is low—and while the majority of students are Latino, Asian, or African American, a majority of those who vote in school elections and most school board members are non-Hispanic whites.

Funding for education fell during the Great Recession, but climbed to $77 billion in 2014–2015. The state supplied 60 percent of the funds (over 40 percent of the state budget), the federal government provided 9 percent, and the rest came from local taxes and other local sources.[5] As we learned in Chapter 8, however, California ranks poorly among the states on per-pupil spending and quality of education. Per-pupil funding varies greatly among the state's many school districts, however. Rich districts may spend twice as much per student as poor districts. Governor Brown's 2013 **Local Control Funding Formula** addressed this by increasing funding for districts with high-needs students and generally reducing state controls on school district spending.

Almost all of this money goes to salaries and operating expenses. Funding for building repairs and construction of new schools comes mostly from **bonds** (borrowed money paid by local taxes), which require approval by a supermajority of voters (55 percent)—and usually get it. The state also sometimes issues construction bonds—also with voter approval—and distributes the funds to local school districts.

Special districts are an even more ubiquitous form of local government, with no fewer than 5,141 in California. Unlike cities and counties, which are "general-purpose" governments, special districts provide a single service. California law provides for fifty-three different types of special districts, ranging from water and waste disposal districts to hospital and cemetery districts. They are created when citizens or governments want a particular function performed but have no appropriate agency to provide the service or prefer not to delegate it to a city or county. Sometimes special districts are formed when small communities share responsibilities for fire protection, sewage treatment, or other services that can be more efficiently provided cooperatively. When **Proposition 13**

passed in 1978, the number of special districts increased because the initiative imposed tax constraints on general-purpose local governments (cities and counties) and local leaders found it easier to fund some services through special districts. Funding usually comes from property taxes or charges for the service the district provides.

City councils or county boards of supervisors govern some special districts, but most are overseen by commissions or boards of directors that may be elected or appointed by other officials. Like school boards, these bodies appoint professional administrators to manage their work. Accountability to the voters and taxpayers is minimal, however, because most of us aren't even aware of these officials.

Coping with So Many Governments

All these different types of local governments operate in every urban region of California. The vast urban areas between Los Angeles and San Diego or around San Francisco Bay, for example, consist of many cities, counties, and special districts, with no single authority in charge of the whole region. Los Angeles County alone hosts eighty-eight cities and nearly 300 special districts. This **fragmentation** of urban areas into so many governing entities may make local government more accessible to citizens, but it can be costly because governing agencies are sometimes too small to provide services efficiently. More seriously, fragmentation makes it difficult to deal with problems such as transportation and air pollution that go far beyond the boundaries of any one entity.

Some cities deal with this situation by **contracting for services** from counties, larger cities, or private businesses. In Los Angeles County, for example, cities can pay the county to provide services ranging from dog catching to tree planting. Small cities commonly contract with the county sheriff for police protection rather than fund their own forces. Contracting allows such communities to provide needed services while retaining local control, although some see the system as unfair because wealthy communities can afford more than poor ones.

Another solution to urban fragmentation is **consolidation**, or the merger of existing governmental entities. With voter approval, small school districts, special districts, or even cities can unite to provide services more efficiently. In the past, consolidation has occurred mostly with school districts, but proposals for consolidations have become more common lately because of California's prolonged budget crisis.

Special districts are another way to address fragmentation and regional problems—particularly problems, such as air pollution and transportation, which extend beyond the boundaries of existing cities or counties. For example, California has dozens of transit districts that run bus and rail systems. Most are countywide, but some, including Bay Area Rapid Transit (BART), cover several counties.

The state has attempted to encourage cooperation among multiple governments in urban regions by requiring the development of regional plans for housing, jobs, and transportation through **councils of governments (COGs)** in which all of the cities and counties in the regions are represented. Two major COGs are the Southern California Association of Governments (SCAG) and the nine-county Association of Bay Area Governments (ABAG) in northern California. Other state-created agencies, such as the Metropolitan Water District and the South Coast Air Quality Management Board in southern California, exercise regional power that goes well beyond planning.

DIRECT DEMOCRACY IN LOCAL POLITICS

As in state politics, direct democracy is a fixture of local government in California. An average of nearly 400 local ballot measures are voted on by Californians each year. Recall elections for local officials are also possible, but with only fourteen in 2015, a fairly typical year, they're rare.[6] Most ballot measures are charter amendments—such as increasing the powers of the mayor or introducing district council elections—or proposals to introduce or raise taxes or to borrow money by issuing bonds; these must also win voter approval. Charter changes require a simple majority, but bonds and most tax increases require a two-thirds supermajority, which has severely restricted the ability of local governments to raise money, because voters are usually reluctant to increase taxes.

What are referred to as propositions on statewide ballots are called "measures" at the local level. Most are placed on the ballot by a city council, county board of supervisors, or school board. Tax measures are most common, especially for school districts, followed by charter amendments. Citizens also put proposals to the voters through the initiative process, although initiatives constitute only 2 percent of local measures. Most often, the initiatives are attempts to control growth or amend charters. Recent local initiatives have addressed rent control, fracking as a means of oil extraction, and taxes on sugary drinks.

In the 1970s and 1980s, residents of some cities, usually allied with environmentalists, worried that rapid growth spread city services too thinly and resorted to initiatives to limit new development. More recently, the reverse is occurring as developers use initiatives to speed approval of projects, paying signature gatherers to qualify their proposals for the ballot. Once sufficient signatures are collected, state law allows city councils to approve a project without referring it to the voters. If a city council does so, the project is exempt from lawsuits under the California Environmental Quality Act—a mechanism frequently used by environmentalists and other groups to kill or delay projects. Walmart has used this process in nine cities in California, winning council approval in eight without going to the voters.[7]

LOCAL BUDGETS

With California cities spending nearly $70 billion a year and counties spending nearly $65 billion, these budgets combined exceed the general fund budget of the state—serious money! The way that money is raised and spent reveals a great deal about what local governments do and also about their limitations.

The biggest single source of money for California's local governments was once the **property tax**, an annual assessment based on the value of land and buildings. Then, in 1978, taxpayers revolted with **Proposition 13**, a statewide initiative that cut property tax revenues by 57 percent.[8] Today, property taxes provide less than 10 percent of city funds. After drastically cutting services, many cities attempted to compensate for lost revenues by introducing or increasing **charges for services** such as sewage treatment, trash collection, building permits, and the use of recreational facilities. At over 40 percent of all city revenues, such charges are now the largest source of income for most cities. Local governments also came to rely more on sales taxes. Two percent of the state's 7.5 percent sales tax goes to the cities and counties where the sale occurs, and an additional 1 percent goes to counties as compensation for **realignment** (the transfer of some state-provided services to counties). With voter approval, some cities and counties add to the base sales tax to fund transportation or other services, while others have added taxes on hotel rooms, utilities, or other things such as the sale of medical marijuana. Altogether, however, sales tax revenues account for less than 10 percent of local government funds.

The shift from property taxes to other sources of revenue also affected local land use decisions. When a new development is proposed, most cities now prefer retail businesses to housing or industry because of the sales taxes that such businesses generate. This trend has been labeled the **fiscalization of land use** because instead of choosing the best use for the land, cities opt for the one that produces the most revenue. Housing, especially affordable housing, almost never falls into this category. Along with local growth controls, fiscalization of land use contributes substantially to the inadequate supply and high price of housing in California.

With more legal constraints on their taxing powers, counties had an even rougher time after Proposition 13. State aid to counties increased slightly, but with no alternative local taxes readily available after the passage of Proposition 13, most counties cut spending deeply. Like cities, most also increased charges and fees for services, but while the fiscal picture for most counties has improved recently, some are worried that Governor Brown's realignment of responsibilities will further strain their resources.

About half of county revenues come from the state and federal governments (32 percent and 17 percent, respectively), but this money must be spent on required programs such as social services, health care, and the courts. Intergovernmental aid does not cover the cost of these mandatory services, however, leaving counties with little money to spend as they choose. Property taxes and charges for services are other major sources of funding for counties.

Just as the revenue sources of cities and counties differ, so do spending patterns, largely because the state assigns them different responsibilities. Public safety—police and fire protection—is the biggest expenditure for California cities, while the top spending programs for counties are social services and public protection (sheriff, jails, fire, and courts).

Budget Woes

Proposition 13 is much loved by homeowners for reducing property tax bills, but the initiative caused serious fiscal problems for local governments by cutting property tax revenues and making approval of new taxes or tax increases more difficult. Beyond the resulting budget cuts, Proposition 13 gave the state the responsibility to allocate property taxes among local governments even as **Proposition 98** (see Chapter 8) mandated allocation of a fixed percentage of the state budget to education. As a consequence, a portion of property taxes that had previously gone to cities and counties was shifted to schools—putting even further pressure on city and county budgets and resulting in further cuts in services. Ultimately, cities and counties, which previously had some control of their own revenues, became dependent on the state for property and sales tax revenues, a significant loss of local control.

These problems were compounded by recessions in the early 1990s and again in 2001–2003 and 2007–2010. Property values declined, and property tax revenues for local governments fell—along with sales tax revenues. The state exacerbated circumstances for local governments in 2004 by drastically reducing vehicle license fees, previously a significant source of local revenues. In 2009, facing a continued deficit, the state resorted to a massive "take-back" of local property tax revenues, diverting nearly $4 billion in local property taxes from schools, cities, and counties.

Frustrated by all this, cities and counties pushed back with ballot measures to prevent state take-backs and transfers and to guarantee future revenues. Voters approved propositions designed to do this in 2004 and 2010, and the state is now somewhat more constrained. Take-backs can still occur, but the state must eventually repay the funds. Nevertheless, in the short term, the take-backs only worsened the fiscal problems of local governments.

All of this has driven some California cities and counties to the fiscal brink. Oakland and other cities have laid off hundreds of police officers, despite rising crime rates. Maywood, in southern California, laid off all its city employees, including police officers, and contracted with other cities for some services and with Los Angeles County for police protection. Other cities also increased **contracting for services**. San Jose "outsourced" graffiti abatement and some maintenance work. Redding, in northern California, and Santa Clarita, in southern California, contracted with a private company to provide library services.

Many cities and other local agencies also face fiscal strain because of the pensions and other benefits they offered their employees when their budgets were flush with cash. Now unable to meet these commitments but bound by contracts, local governments have sought to renegotiate contracts to win concessions from current employees or to move to a two-tier pension system, preserving benefits for current workers but reducing them for future hires. Voters in Modesto, Palo Alto, San Diego, San Francisco, and San Jose overwhelmingly approved pension reform, but the problem persists and pensions take up an ever-growing portion of local budgets—money that might otherwise fund police, libraries, and other local services.

More drastically, some cities, including Vallejo (near San Francisco) in 2008 and San Bernardino and Stockton in 2012, have declared bankruptcy. Unable to pay employee salaries or repay bonded indebtedness, bankruptcy allowed these cities to legally suspend payments and renegotiate contracts while a bankruptcy judge determines which creditors (including pensions) should be paid. In all cases, city services, including public safety, were cut drastically. Unique circumstances in each of these cities contributed to their dire straits, but some observers worried that bankruptcies would spread to other California cities.

Many cities sought new revenues in various ways. Some, with voter approval, introduced a small local sales tax. San Francisco gave big tax breaks to companies like Twitter for locating in the city, but created a backlash among local residents when affluent "techies" drove up housing costs. Among the techies are Google employees who take a company bus to their jobs in Silicon Valley—resulting in "Google bus" protests when they used municipal bus stops. The new jobs and residents helped San Francisco's tax base, but longtime residents felt threatened by the change.[9]

LOCAL GOVERNMENT IN PERSPECTIVE

The fiscal threat to some local governments has diminished somewhat, but many still struggle with state limits on revenues and increasing costs for services and pensions. Despite these challenges, local governments continue to innovate, from restrictions on smoking to taxes on soda drinks, rent control, and affordable housing. San Francisco launched the movement for same-sex marriage and, with Los Angeles and other cities, increased the minimum wage. Over 150 California cities and counties banned plastic bags before the state was inspired to follow suit, as it often does with locally initiated policies. Maybe that's why opinion polls consistently report that Californians view local government more favorably than state government. Whatever its limitations, California's political system gives residents many opportunities to decide what sort of communities they want, and many Californians take advantage of these opportunities by engaging in local politics.

NOTES

1. See Paul G. Lewis. *Deep Roots: Local Government Structure in California*. San Francisco: Public Policy Institute of California, 1998.

2. Zoltan L. Hajnal, Paul G. Lewis, and Hugh Louch, *Municipal Elections in California: Turnout, Timing, and Competition*. San Francisco: Public Policy Institute of California, March 2002.

3. Jessica Trounstine and Zoltan Hajnal, "Low Voter Turnout Does Matter: Spending Priorities in Local Politics," paper presented at the annual meeting of the Midwest Political Science Association, Chicago, April 2004.

4. Hajnal, Lewis, and Louch, *Municipal Elections*.

5. "Who Pays?" Ed100, http://ed100.org/support/whopays/ (accessed July 14, 2016).

6. California Elections Data Archive, Institute for Social Research, California State University, Sacramento, www.csus.edu/isr (accessed July 15, 2016).

7. "Builders Pierce California's Environmental Shield with New Weapon: The Ballot," *New York Times*, June 7, 2016.

8. See Jack Citrin and Isaac William Martin, eds., *After the Tax Revolt: California's Proposition 13 Turns 30*. Berkeley: Institute of Government Studies, 2009.

9. See Nathan Heller, "California Screaming," *The New Yorker*, July 7 and 14, 2014.

LEARN MORE ON THE WEB

California Elections Data Archive (CEDA) has information on local elections:
    www.csus.edu/isr

For information on counties, go to California State Association of Counties:
    www.csac.counties.org

California State Controller collects data on cities, counties, schools, and special districts:
    www.sco.ca.gov

For more on cities, check out the League of California Cities:
    www.cacities.org

Public Policy Institute of California publishes excellent studies on local government:
    www.ppic.org

GET INVOLVED

The best way to learn about local politics is through an internship or by volunteering with the office of a city council member or county supervisor. Go to your city or county's website to find the elected officials, and contact one of them. You can also intern with a community group—just search the Internet for one that interests you.

10

State–Federal Relations: Conflict, Cooperation, and Chaos

LEARNING OBJECTIVES

10.1 Explore California's clout with Congress.

10.2 Debate high-speed rail.

10.3 Focus on immigration.

10.4 Examine climate change.

10.5 Describe the struggle over water.

10.6 Assess California's shared resources.

California is the most populated state in the United States, with an economy equal to the sixth wealthiest nation in the world. It wasn't always this way. For more than a century, during the 1800s and early 1900s, political observers marveled at Maine as the bellwether of the nation in national elections: "As Maine goes, so goes the nation," the saying went.

These days, the nation looks west to California, for what happens here often indicates what's to come elsewhere. Whether concerns center on resources, infrastructure, ethnic diversity, or technological trends, the management of these and other questions by Californians often serves as a futuristic laboratory for the rest of the nation. The women's right-to-choose movement, gun control, the tax revolt, medical marijuana, stem cell research, and same-sex marriage all had early beginnings—and, in some cases, origins—in California. And so it is with the state's rollercoaster-like relationship with the federal government, which can be described as wary, uneven, often fraught with controversy, and yet necessary.

Sometimes state and national leaders differ over California's management. For example, over the years, federal officials and state leaders have tussled over the best way to respond to administering the state's unpredictable water supply and prison management. On other issues, however, such as California's implementation of the Affordable Care Act, the two governments have worked in a seamless fashion. There are also instances in which California has led the way in responding to national issues, with the federal government eventually moving into line; nowhere is this more obvious than with environmental protection, particularly air pollution. Deciding the best responses to problems that affect both the nation and state can be a challenge because, like its forty-nine counterparts, California is both a self-governing entity and a member of the union.

Matters become even more complicated when determining financial responsibility for costly issues such as massive transportation projects and control of undocumented immigration. Because the state is so large and complex, federal support in these areas almost always appears inadequate. More times than not, when federal programs are cut, California seems to suffer disproportionately compared with other states.

This chapter chronicles California's impact on national policy making and policy actors. It includes some of the most important policy areas that define, and sometimes test, California's relationship with the federal government: high-speed rail, immigration, climate change, water, and the distribution of federal resources. Each topic touches on the delicate balance between state autonomy and national objectives—perspectives in federalism that are not always viewed the same ways by state and federal government leaders.

CALIFORNIA'S CLOUT WITH THE PRESIDENT

Despite its size and huge bloc of Electoral College votes, California hasn't figured prominently in presidential elections in recent years, largely because the state has been reliably secure for Democratic candidates on every occasion since 1992. Candidates don't appear here as much as they do in other states, where the outcomes are uncertain. But California is important to candidates of both national political parties as the top state for campaign contributions. That alone keeps candidates coming to places such as Orange County, Silicon Valley, and Hollywood frequently, year in and year out. But campaign contributions and electoral votes don't necessarily equate with attention.

California has had an uneven relationship with the nation's presidents. For example, Republican President George W. Bush was not particularly helpful to the state largely because of his hands-off attitude on domestic policy issues. Differences between the Bush administration and California public officials existed over agriculture, border patrol assistance, environmental protection, terrorism funding, and responsibility for a nearly cataclysmic electricity shortage in 2001.

President Barack Obama was somewhat more responsive to California's issues, particularly with respect to support for environmental matters, "green" technology research and production, and the state's strict rules on automobile exhaust emissions. On implementation of the Affordable Care Act, the Obama administration provided more than $1 billion to create Covered California.[1] During the first year, California cut the number of uninsured residents in half and signed up 1.5 million residents, nearly 18 percent of the national total of 8 million enrollees. Still, there were areas of disagreement. The Obama administration compensated California for only a fraction of the hundreds of millions of dollars spent by the state on the incarceration of undocumented immigrants awaiting deportation. And California received very little of Obama's "Race to the Top" education improvement funds. But on balance, California had more success with President Obama than with his predecessor.

Because California is such a blue state, most of the state's public officials viewed the election of Hillary Clinton as a positive sign for increased federal attention. Many of her campaign themes resonated with the California leaders, giving hope that there would be more federal assistance for public education, infrastructure, technology, and health care and immigration reform. But the surprise election of Republican Donald Trump to the presidency erased those expectations, as well as long-awaited immigration reform. No doubt, some of these solutions will require the help of Congress.

CALIFORNIA'S CLOUT WITH CONGRESS

As the nation's most populated state, California has fifty-three members in the House of Representatives, dwarfing the delegations of every other state. Texas and New York are second and third, with thirty-two and twenty-nine members, respectively. The majority party in each chamber of Congress chooses committee chairs who, in turn, manage the flow of legislation.

The twenty-first century began with Republicans enjoying control of both houses. In 2006, growing discontent with the war in Iraq, an uneven national economy, and political corruption in Congress led the nation's voters to elect a Democratic majority to the House of Representatives. San Francisco's **Nancy Pelosi**, minority leader since 2002, was elected speaker, the highest national leadership post ever held in the United States by a woman. With that election outcome, several prominent California Democrats assumed key committee chairmanships by virtue of their years of seniority in the House.

Political party fortunes turned in 2010 when the Republicans captured control of the House, which continued through the 2016 elections, albeit with a slimmer margin. As a result, two California Republicans have enjoyed key committee chairmanships, including the Committee on Intelligence (Devin Nunes) and Committee on Foreign Affairs (Edward Royce). In addition, in 2014, **Kevin McCarthy** was elected majority leader, the highest leadership post after speaker.

Democrats in California enjoy a comfortable margin of 39–14 over Republicans in the House of Representatives. In other respects, California's congressional makeup is as diverse as the rest of the state. As of 2017, the delegation includes 12 Latinos, 3 African Americans, 6 Asian Americans, 17 females, and one openly gay member. Both of California's U.S. senators are women as well.

The political winds have shifted in the U.S. Senate where, as with the House, the majority party controls all committee chairmanships and the flow of legislation. In 2006, the off-year revolution produced a Democratic majority.

With that change, California Senators **Dianne Feinstein** and **Barbara Boxer** both became committee chairs. But Republicans reclaimed the majority in 2014, costing Boxer her position as chair of the Environment and Public Works Committee, and Feinstein her position as chair of the influential Select Committee on Intelligence. The change in Senate control signified reduced clout for California. After the 2016 election, Republicans maintained a majority and therefore all the committee chairmanships. Their unexpected success reflected the national surge for Trump. Within the state, California Attorney General and Democrat **Kamala Harris** was elected to replace retiring Democrat Barbara Boxer.

One other fact must be added to the discussion of Californians in Washington: historically, California's **congressional delegation** has been notoriously fractured on key public policy issues affecting California. Much of the conflict stems from the state's complexity. North/south, urban/suburban/rural, and coastal/valley/mountain divisions separate the state geographically. Other differences exist, too, in terms of wealth, ethnicity, and basic liberal/conservative distinctions. To be sure, no congressional district is completely homogeneous, yet most members of Congress tend to protect their districts' interests more than those of the state as a whole. Thus, on issues ranging from desert protection to water policy to immigration reform, California's representatives have often canceled each other's votes, leaving states such as Texas far more powerful because of their relatively unified stances. Even on foreign trade, members from California often have worked at cross-purposes, depending on the industries, interest groups, and demographic characteristics of their districts. Only on the question of offshore oil drilling have most members of the state's delegation voted the same way in opposition to the proposal.

HIGH-SPEED RAIL

In 2008, California voters passed **Proposition 1A**, which committed $9.95 billion in bonds to partially fund an 800-mile-long San Diego–to–San Francisco high-speed rail system. Officially known as the Safe, Reliable High-Speed Passenger Train Bond Act for the 21st Century, the ballot proposition was the down payment of a transportation system projected to cost $43 billion. Proponents touted the rail network as an environmentally friendly enterprise equivalent to the addition of twelve polluting highway lanes up and down the length of the state. They envisioned not only a federal/state partnership but also collaboration between the state and the private sector.

The Obama administration gushed over the transportation network as a twenty-first-century infrastructure gem and immediately made available $3.3 billion in matching federal funds for the first segment of construction, which would span the 130-mile stretch between Chowchilla and Bakersfield. In July 2012, the legislature committed the first $2.7 billion of the 2008 bond to begin work, originally scheduled for the fall of 2012.

Meanwhile, critics began to express doubts about the project. In 2011, a new study revised the cost upward to $99 billion and predicted fewer riders.[2] Leaders in the now Republican-led House of Representatives also balked at providing federal funds. Ironically, the opposition effort was led by two Californians, Central Valley–based Jeff Denham, who voted for the project earlier as a state legislator, and Kevin McCarthy, the then-House majority whip from Bakersfield, who became House majority leader in 2014.[3]

In 2012, the High-Speed Rail Commission, the project's governing author-ity, produced a new plan that cut the cost of the transportation system to $68 billion. But that did little to assuage the growing number of opponents. The nonpartisan Legislative Analyst's Office urged lawmakers to terminate the effort. Public opinion polls found the voters now wanting to vote again on the idea, with sizable numbers against it. Still, Governor **Jerry Brown** remained support-ive. In 2014, the legislature and Governor Brown agreed to commit a minimum of $250 million annually for high-speed rail from cap-and-trade revenues pro-duced by **AB 32**, the state's **Global Warming Solutions Act**. Supporters received more good news in 2014, when a new study estimated that ridership would be 25 percent higher than originally forecast, putting a damper on claims that the project would not be economically feasible.[4]

In January 2015, the state broke ground on the first leg of construction. Yet, credibility issues persisted over costs and construction priorities. In 2016, the High-Speed Rail Commission produced a revised plan that would first link Bakersfield to San Jose, instead of connecting Bakersfield to Los Angeles, as orig-inally intended. The new construction route would save $4 billion, according to the authority.[5]

Countless questions remain about the high-speed rail program. Lawsuits over property rights, funding sources, the projected route, environmental concerns, and other issues have slowed progress. There are also other pressing questions. Will the new Trump administration help California's high speed rail program as part of its commitment to rebuild the nation's infrastructure? Will Republican Majority Leader Kevin McCarthy soften his funding opposition, given the new administra-tion? And if not, can the state generate enough funds to pay for the system? For now, the outcome of this story remains a mystery.

IMMIGRATION

California has long been a magnet for those in search of opportunity. And they have come—first Spanish; then Yankee, Irish, and Chinese immigrants during the nineteenth century; followed by Japanese, Eastern European, African Ameri-can, and, later, Vietnamese immigrants beginning in the 1970s, Asian Indians in the 1990s, and more Latinos throughout the past half century (see Table 10.1). But over the past two decades, several factors have converged to influence the moods of the state's residents and would-be residents. Lack of opportunity in other nations has led millions to choose California as an alternative; meanwhile, economic uncertainty fueled by globalization has led many of those already here to oppose further immigration. Much of the antipathy has been directed at Latinos—particularly those from Mexico—but anger has also been aimed at Asians.

TABLE 10.1 **California's Immigrants: Leading Countries of Origin, 2011**

Country	Number
Mexico	4,263,404
Philippines	820,280
China (including Taiwan)	506,810
Vietnam	488,572
El Salvador	423,569

SOURCE: California Department of Finance.

The numbers are substantial. Whereas in 1980, 15.1 percent of California's population was foreign-born, 27.1 percent fell within that category in 2014. During the same period, the percentage of foreign-born residents of the United States as a whole nearly doubled, from 6.2 percent to 13.1 percent (see Figure 10.1). In 2014, the Pew Hispanic Center estimated that there were 11.2 million undocumented immigrants nationwide;[6] about 2.67 million resided in California, making it the state with the largest population of undocumented residents.[7]

Experts have argued about whether the immigrants help or harm the state's economy. As of 2014, more than 1 million undocumented immigrants in California were denied health insurance through the Affordable Care Act, presenting a financial burden for public health institutions and services.[8] Yet other studies show that immigrants, both legal and undocumented, are very similar in economic makeup to the rest of the United States.[9] Moreover, undocumented immigrants are critical to some industries, such as California farming, a $48 billion economy where they comprise as much as 90 percent of the harvest workforce. On this note, in 2013, U.S. Senator Dianne Feinstein asked the Department of Homeland Security (DHS) to cease deportation of illegal farm workers in California inasmuch as their departure would severely harm the state's agricultural economy.[10] Since then, the DHS has paid less attention to deporting farm workers, although no formal change in policy has been announced.

Before and after Feinstein's request, the federal government has continued to act on illegal immigration, although not always with consistency. In 2008, the Bush administration increased surveillance of U.S. companies with undocumented immigrant employees, leading to fines for employers, deportation for undocumented workers, and workforce shortages. Between a more vigilant border protection system and a declining U.S. economy, the number of attempted border crossings by illegal immigrants declined, and more than 1 million undocumented immigrants returned to their home countries by 2010.

The Obama administration was also erratic on the immigration issue. From his earliest days in office, President Obama pressed Congress for comprehensive immigration reform that provided a path to citizenship for law-abiding undocumented residents, but members of Congress could not agree on a program. Meanwhile, the administration periodically continued selective deportation of undocumented residents.[11] Yet, in 2014, President Obama announced an executive order that allowed

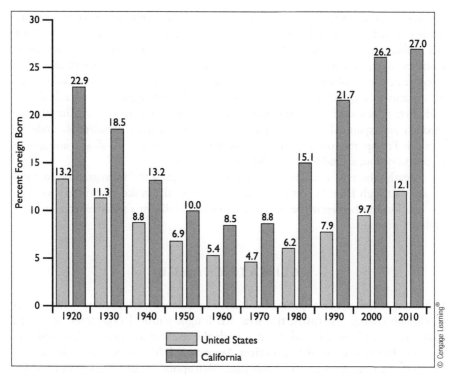

F I G U R E   10.1   Population of Foreign-Born Residents, California and United States Comparison.

as many as 5 million undocumented parents and their American-born children the ability to remain in the United States for at least three years. That move was squelched by the courts, but the issue is far from resolved.

The largest issue related to immigration is determining which level of government should assume responsibility for its costs. While the federal government has long established the criteria for immigration and the conditions for enforcement, it leaves the states responsible for meeting the needs of immigrants. Nowhere does this contradiction ring louder than in California. One 2014 study reported that undocumented immigrants and their children cost the state more than $25 billion annually, including estimated health care costs of $4 billion, education costs for more than 1 million children at $14.4 billion, and incarceration costs of $4.4 billion.[12] Yet another study by the Congressional Budget Office found that the "net impact of the unauthorized population on state and local budgets … is most likely modest."[13] Clearly, there are disagreements over costs and benefits.

Recent changes in California indicate considerably more acceptance of immigrants than thirty years ago, when the voters made English the state's official language and attempted to deny all government benefits to illegal immigrants. In 2011, Governor Brown signed into law the California Dream Act, which allowed illegal immigrants attending public colleges and universities to receive state financial aid. In 2013, Governor Brown signed the Trust Act, which prevents local law enforcement authorities from keeping illegal immigrants in custody any more than necessary, making it more difficult for federal authorities to seize them. In the same year, the legislature passed and the governor signed a bill permitting illegal immigrants to acquire driver's licenses. In 2015, Brown signed the Health for All Kids Act, which enabled all undocumented children to gain access to health care through an expanded Medi-Cal program. Yet Republican presidential candidate Donald Trump ran on a platform dedicated to removing all illegal immigrants from the nation, including 2.7 million in California.

Clearly, the role of each government in managing the immigration question remains a tough issue to sort out. Nevertheless, in the wake of Trump's victory, the relationship between the new president and California's leaders appears on a collision course.

CLIMATE CHANGE

California and the federal government have had a rocky relationship with respect to climate change. At times, the state has fought national objectives; at others, California has taken the lead. So it is with the issue of air quality. According to the U.S. **Environmental Protection Agency (EPA)**, the ten smoggiest counties in the nation are found in California. Metropolitan Los Angeles, an area that extends east to Riverside and south to Long Beach, tops the list as the smoggiest area in the nation. Actually, the number of "unhealthful" days in the Los Angeles basin declined from an average of 189.6 between 1996–1998 to 141.8 between 2006 and 2008, according to the American Lung Association, although progress has slowed since 2004.[14] Still, statewide, the costs continue to be sizable. A 2011 study found that motor vehicle exhausts alone accounted for up to $8 billion annually in the form of premature deaths, respiratory illnesses, and lost productivity in the workplace.[15]

Congress and the EPA have been unhappy with the state's slow action on clean air. But given the state's manufacturing sector, particularly in the vast Los Angeles basin, it has been difficult to meet national standards without choking off the local economy. In 1992 state regulators established the Regional Clean Air Incentives Market Program (RECLAIM) in southern California, a program in which manufacturers buy and sell emissions permits as a means of encouraging emissions reduction and moving away from fossil fuels. The concept was expanded in 2012 when the state Air Resources Board began selling greenhouse gas pollution credits to companies exceeding allotted pollution limits. The first year's sale of "cap and trade" permits brought in $290 million. However, experts believe that the state will soon be collecting more than $2 billion annually, with emissions reduced to 1990 levels by 2020, as required by the legislation.[16]

California has been very ambitious with electricity. In 2011, the legislature passed a law requiring one-third of the state's electricity to come from renewable sources such as solar, wind, and hydroelectric production by 2020. After initial protests, the state's major energy suppliers met and exceeded their targets. In 2015, Governor Brown moved the bar with his signature on legislation requiring state utilities to generate 50 percent of electricity from renewables by 2030.

Automobile exhaust is another story, however. California has led the nation in reducing auto emissions, which account for 28 percent of the state's greenhouse gases. Since the passage of the federal Clean Air Act of 1970, state environmental regulators had asked for and received forty-four waivers from the EPA to exceed federal requirements. That's what happened routinely until 2007, when the Bush administration's EPA rejected the claim that auto emissions contained greenhouse gases, California and sixteen other states sued the EPA for not carrying out its mandate. The U.S. Supreme Court agreed.

The political environment regarding auto emissions changed dramatically with the election of Barack Obama to the presidency in 2008. Early in June 2009, his new EPA administrator approved California's proposal and announced it would be a new national policy by 2017. On this occasion, at least, California has set the trend. More changes followed. In 2015, the California Air Resources Board approved a new regulation requiring all oil producers to eliminate 10 percent of the carbon in transportation fuels by 2020. In the same year, the federal EPA adopted stricter air quality limits, reducing the 75 parts per million (ppm) ozone standard established by the Bush administration to 70 ppm.

Manufacturers screamed that the new rules would put California out of business, but health experts claimed that the new rules would prevent hundreds of thousands of asthma attacks and hundreds of deaths from cardiovascular diseases and other respiratory-related diseases. More importantly, on the issue of climate change, the state and federal governments were finally on the same page.

In his 2016 campaign, presidential candidate Donald Trump described climate change as a "hoax." Given his concerns with alternative energy and support for more fossil fuels, the new national energy policy may well clash with the direction of the Golden State.

WATER

Not all of California's jurisdictional disputes have occurred with the federal government. On the issue of water, California repeatedly has tangled with other states. Simply put, the state doesn't have enough. Three-quarters of California's water comes from north of Sacramento, while 80 percent is consumed south of Sacramento. Most of the imbalance is corrected through two giant transfer systems. The federal Central Valley Project, which dates from 1937, supplies the farmers of the southern Central Valley. The State Water Project, begun in 1960, largely serves southern urban areas. Both systems intercept freshwater near the Sacramento–San Joaquin Delta before it can flow through the delta out to the ocean. Still, California gasps for more water, which has led to confrontations with other states and, to a lesser degree, the federal government.

The linchpin of the water frenzy among western states is the Colorado River, the freshwater source that begins in Colorado and empties into the Gulf of California. Under a 1922 multistate agreement, California is entitled to 4.4 million acre-feet, or 59 percent, of the lower basin river annually. Yet, by the end of the twentieth century, California exceeded its share by as much as 800,000 acre-feet per year, enough to provide for the annual water needs of 1.6 million households in rapidly growing Arizona and Nevada.[17] In 2000, officials from the seven states agreed to a formula that would allow California to gradually reduce its consumption of the excess over a fifteen-year period.

Meanwhile, the federal government's Department of the Interior and the State of California mediated the ongoing three-way battle among agribusiness (which typically consumes as much as 80 percent of the state's water), environmentalists seeking to preserve rivers and deltas, and urban areas. The two governments developed a plan in 2000 to expand existing federal reservoirs in California, improve drinking-water quality, and develop a creative water-recycling program. Most of the $8.5 billion price tag has been shouldered by the federal government, with Californians providing $825 million. In 2004, Congress committed another $10 billion over thirty years to improve the quality of water flowing into the Sacramento Delta and San Francisco Bay.

Improving the quality of California's water is important, but assuring enough quantity is equally vital to the state's wellbeing. On this score, the prognosis is not good. Between 1970 and 2015, the population of the state doubled. Meanwhile, between a reduced allocation from the Colorado River and the state's fickle climatological conditions, the water supply has become increasingly unreliable. That's because the state depends upon the annual Sierra Nevada snowpack for as much as 60 percent of its water. But when the state succumbs to drought, the lack of water can cause economic havoc. One such period occurred between 2006 and 2009, which was declared a moderate drought. However, that paled compared to 2011–2015, when California encountered the worst drought in memory. By one account, the drought forced farmers to leave 1.03 million acres fallow, or about 15 percent of the state's cropland.[18] Another study in 2015 projected costs to agriculture of $2.7 billion and 18,600 jobs.[19] Clearly, the drought has extracted a huge price.

The state has long-term water problems, too. Because of few regulations, many farmers have relied more than ever on groundwater sources to make up for the shortfall from Sierra runoffs. As such, they are taking out about 2 million more acre-feet each year than they recharge, depleting the state's underground water table in the process.[20] In addition, large swaths of the Central Valley operate without water meters, which makes it impossible to assess the use or abuse of water. The voters passed a $7.5 billion water bond (Proposition 1) on the ballot in November 2014, but the bond, while financing new long-term storage, offered little immediate relief.

In 2012, Governor Jerry Brown laid out plans to divert additional water from the Sacramento Delta through what he termed a "peripheral tunnel" in an effort to meet the state's growing needs. No sooner had the governor delivered his announcement than environmental groups and several members of the California congressional delegation protested over sacrificing the delta to meet the needs of water-greedy farmers. As with the "peripheral canal" proposed by Brown 35 years earlier, this plan also was caught in the continuing dispute between the state's major water interests, with little likelihood of agreement in the near future.

Meanwhile, the state struggled to deal with what became a crisis. In early 2015, Governor Jerry Brown issued an executive order mandating a 25 percent reduction in water use. Over the next twelve months, Californians came close to meeting the mandate. A close-to-normal rainy season the following year allowed the governor to lessen the reduction mandate slightly to 20 percent.

Some local governments have turned to desalination plants, such as the $1 billion operation in Carlsbad now providing 50,000 gallons daily for 400,000 residents. Better use of recycled water and replacement of urban lawns with drought-resistant plants are also potential remedies. But with agriculture consuming as much as 80 percent of the state's water, farmers also may need to rethink the crops they grow as well as their current methods of irrigation. This problem is not likely to go away soon.

For the moment, California will have to rely on its own resources to manage its water issues. That became clear in 2016, when on a campaign swing through Fresno, then-candidate Donald Trump, rejected any claims of a water shortage in California, thus implying that solutions must be found from within.

SHARED RESOURCES

Federalism refers to the multifaceted political relationship that binds the state and national governments. One aspect centers on financial assistance that wends its way from federal coffers to state and local treasuries; that amounted to about $343 billion in fiscal year 2013. Most of this assistance comes in the form of **grants-in-aid**, amounting to about 20 percent of all state and local government revenues. The money flows through more than 600 federal programs covering areas from agricultural development to high-tech research.

For decades, California received more than its fair share of grants-in-aid from the federal government. That has changed. In 1983, California had 10 percent of the national population but received 22 percent of the national government's expenditures, thanks largely to defense- and space-related research. Then came the slide. With a pared defense budget, cutbacks in infrastructure work, and the push for a balanced budget, federal contributions have shrunk considerably over the past two decades. As of 2013, California had ranked fourteenth among the fifty states in per capita contributions to the national government, but fortieth in per capita dollars received from the federal government.

There is another way to appreciate the changing relationship between the federal government and California. Because of the state's massive growth, California had a long history of getting more dollars from the federal government than it contributed. Beginning in 1986, however, California became a "donor" state. Ever since, California has contributed more money to the national treasury than it has received, and the disparity is increasing every year. In 1992, for every dollar California sent to Washington, D.C., the state received 93 cents in federal goods and services. By 2013, for every dollar California sent to Washington, only

T A B L E 10.2 Federal Expenditures per Dollar of Taxes, Fiscal Years 1992 and 2013—California and Selected States

State	Expenditures per Dollar of Taxes		Ranking	
	FY1992	FY2013	FY1992	FY2013
New Mexico	$2.08	$2.19	11	4
Texas	0.93	0.79	37	30
Massachusetts	1.01	0.74	31	33
California	0.93	0.68	38	36
Kansas	1.05	0.54	27	42
Maryland	1.27	0.23	15	50

SOURCE: Tax Foundation, Bureau of Economic Analysis, Internal Revenue Service.

68 cents came back in goods and services (see Table 10.2). Even when California and the rest of the states received a larger federal commitment from the Economic Recovery and Reinvestment Act in 2009 and 2010, the state's share ranked in the bottom half of the per capita federal expenditures. No matter how you slice it, California is getting less of the federal "pie" today than in the past.[21]

But there is more to the story than just dollars in and dollars out; it's what the dollars buy that makes a huge difference, and in California the high cost of living makes national numbers meaningless. Data compiled in 2015 by United Way found that a family of four in this state needs nearly $68,000 per year to cover basic needs, nearly triple the federal level.[22] And when we consider that the state's immigrant population is more than twice the national average on a per capita basis, it becomes clear that the state's needs fare particularly poorly when it comes to federal funding.

The data presented here show a state that has given much more to the federal government in taxes than it has received in programs and services. They also reflect the fragmentation that has haunted the state's congressional delegation. As a result, California's "Golden State" nickname has a different meaning in Washington than in California—namely, sizable economic resources that have landed disproportionately in the federal treasury.

CALIFORNIA TODAY:
GOLDEN STATE OR FOOL'S GOLD?

Is today's California still the state with unlimited potential or the state with too many burdens to survive? When it comes to relations with the federal government, perhaps the answer is a little of both. California is king when it comes to campaign contributions for national candidates, research and development, agriculture, auto emissions standards, and contributions to the federal treasury. At the same time, California is a pauper in dealing with a perpetually uneven state budget, a dilapidated infrastructure, underfunded public education, a frayed social safety net, and financial help from the federal government. It wasn't always this way, but it is today.

As noted at the beginning of this chapter, some of the shift has been because of the ebb and flow of national politics. Thus, during the Bill Clinton years, the state benefited from extra federal attention on research and development tax credits, H1-B visas for skilled workers, and even some defense contracts. During the George W. Bush years, California didn't fare as well, as attested by the administration's disregard for the state's immigration issues, water management, and electricity crisis.

Under President Obama, California received support for continuation of the research and development tax credit, high-speed rail, and assistance for California homeowners dealing with foreclosure issues. At the same time, federal dollars for public education and recovery from the Great Recession were relatively sparse. Now, President Donald Trump must recommend spending priorities, including the distribution of federal funds to California as well as the other 49 states.

If nothing else, California operates with more financial autonomy from the federal government today than in the times of heavy government defense spending. To this extent the state has experienced a reduced federal reliance, although federal funding to organize the state's Covered California health system was welcome support. Accordingly, California's growing fiscal self-reliance may be the hallmark of the state's direction in the coming years. Whatever the future, it will be an interesting experiment.

NOTES

1. "Covered California Gets Federal Money to Improve Service, Enrollment," *Los Angeles Times*, January 23, 2014, http://articles.latimes.com/2014/jan/23/business/la-fi-california-exchange-20140124.

2. "Forecast Dire for Riders, Revenue," *San Jose Mercury News*, October 11, 2011, pp. A1, A8.

3. "Bullet Train Funds in GOP Sights," *Los Angeles Times*, October 23, 2011, pp. AA1, AA4.

4. "Bullet Train Forecast Updated," *Los Angeles Times*, February 8, 2014, pp. AA1, AA4.

5. "Connecting and Transforming California," Draft 2016 Business Plan, Sacramento, CA, February 23, 2016, www.hsr.ca.gov/docs/about/business_plans/DRAFT_2016_Business_Plan_0201816.pdf.

6. "Statistical Portrait of the Foreign-Born Population in the United States," Pew Hispanic Research Center, September 28, 2015, www.pewhispanic.org/2015/09/28/statistical-portrait-of-the-foreign-born-population-in-the-united-states-1960-2013-key-charts/#2013-fb-unauthorized-line.

7. "Just the Facts: Undocumented Immigrants," Public Policy Institute of California, June 2015, www.ppic.org/main/publication_show.asp?i=818.

8. "Immigrants without Legal Status Remain Mostly in Healthcare Limbo," Los Angeles Times, January 19, 2014, http://articles.latimes.com/2014/jan/19/local/la-me-immigrant-healthcare-20140120.

9. "Immigrants in the Work Force: Study Belies Image," *New York Times*, April 10, 2010, pp. A1, A3.

10. "California Senator Calls for Homeland Security to Stop Deportation of Farmworkers," *Think Progress*, September 6, 2013, http://thinkprogress.org/immigration/2013/09/06/2578321/feinstein-deportation-farmworkers.

11. "Obama Administration Kicks Off Family Deportation Raids," *Politico*, January 6, 2016, www.politico.com/story/2016/01/obama-family-deportation-raids-217329.

12. "Illegal Immigration Costs California More than $25 Billion a Year, Finds FAIR," press release, Federation for American Immigration Reform, June 14, 2014, www.fairus.org/news/illegal-immigration-costs-california-taxpayers-more-than-25-billion-a-year-finds-fair.

13. Quoted in "3 Facts about the Supposed Costs of Undocumented Immigration," *The Nation*, October 12, 2015, www.thenation.com/article/three-facts-about-the-supposed-cost-of-undocumented-immigration/.

14. "Smog in L.A. Still Tops in Nation," *Los Angeles Times*, April 28, 2010, pp. AA1, AA6.

15. "The Road to Clean Air," American Lung Association, 2011, p. 4, www.lung.org/associations/states/california/assets/pdfs/advocacy/clean-cars-campaign/the-road-to-clean-air.pdf.

16. "Cap-Trade's Smooth Start," *Los Angeles Times*, June 14, 2015, pp. C1, C12.

17. "California Water Users Miss Deadline for Pact Sharing," *New York Times*, January 1, 2003. The six states in addition to California are Arizona, Colorado, Nevada, New Mexico, Utah, and Wyoming.

18. "Federal Agencies Release Data Showing California Central Valley Idle Farmland Doubling during Drought," NASA Ames, October 21, 2015, http://landsat.gsfc.nasa.gov/?p=11261.

19. "Drought Takes $2.7 Billion Toll on California Agriculture," *Scientific American*, June 3, 2015, www.scientificamerican.com/article/drought-takes-2-7-billion-toll-on-california-agriculture/.

20. "Regulating Water Wells More Likely than Ever," *San Jose Mercury News*, March 31, 2014, pp. 1, 6.

21. "How Are Federal Dollars Spent in California?" *California Budget Project*, Sacramento, CA, November 2011, p. 7.

22. Betsy Baum Block, Henry Gascon, Peter Manzo, and Adam D. Parker, *Struggling to Get By: The Real Cost Measure to California 2015*: South Pasadena, CA:United Ways of California, 2015, p. 10, www.counties.org/sites/main/files/struggling_to_get_by_2015.pdf.

LEARN MORE ON THE WEB

California and federal taxes:
www.taxfoundation.org

California Institute for Federal Policy Research:
www.calinst.org

Environmental Protection Agency:
  www.epa.gov

Immigration:
  www.irps.ucsd.edu

Office of Management and Budget:
  www.whitehouse.gov/omb

U.S. House of Representatives:
  www.house.gov

U.S. Senate:
  www.senate.gov

GET INVOLVED

Research the votes of your local member of Congress on an issue such as immigration, climate change, or water legislation. How has he or she compared with the rest of the state's delegation, the actual outcome in Congress, or public opinion polls in California?

Glossary

AB 32, Global Warming Solutions Act Legislation requiring polluting companies to purchase cap-and-trade permits that helped to fund programs to protect improve air quality, including the state's high-speed rail project.

annexation The process by which a city adds territory by absorbing adjacent unincorporated areas.

at-large elections City council elections in which all candidates are elected by the community as a whole rather than by districts.

attorney general The state's elected top law enforcement officer and legal counsel; the second-most powerful member of the executive branch.

bicameral legislature Organization of the state legislature into two houses: the forty-member senate (elected for four-year terms) and the eighty-member assembly (elected for two-year terms).

Big Five The governor, assembly speaker, assembly minority leader, senate president pro tem, and senate minority leader, who gather together informally to hash out decisions on the annual budget and other major policy issues.

Board of Equalization The five-member state board that maintains uniform property tax assessments and oversees the

collection of sales, gasoline, and liquor taxes; members are elected by district; part of the executive branch.

board of supervisors The five-member governing body of counties; elected by district to four-year terms.

bonds Subject to voter approval, state and local governments can borrow money by issuing bonds, which are repaid (with interest) from the general fund budget or from special taxes or fees.

Boxer, Barbara U.S. Senator from California first elected in 1992; retired in 2016.

Brown, Edmund G. "Jerry" A Democrat, and California's longest serving governor (1975–1983; 2011–2019).

Brown, Edmund G. "Pat" Prominent Democratic governor (1959–1967) responsible for construction of major infrastructure projects and the state university system.

bureaucracy State or local government workers employed through the civil service system rather than appointed by the governor or other elected officials.

California Dream Act Legislation that allowed illegal immigrants attending public colleges and universities to receive state financial aid.

Cantil-Sakauye, Tani Chief justice of the California Supreme Court (2011–); appointed by Republican governor Arnold Schwarzenegger.

central committees Political party organizations at county and state levels; weakly linked to one another.

charges for services Local government fees for services such as sewage treatment, trash collection, building permits, and the use of recreational facilities; a major source of income for cities and counties since the passage of Proposition 13 in 1978.

charter The equivalent of a constitution for a local government; includes government structures, election systems, powers of officeholders, conditions for employing local government workers, and often much more.

charter city or county A local government that drafts its own structures and organization through a document like a local constitution (also known as a "home rule" charter), subject to voter approval.

Chiang, John California state controller 2007–2015; elected treasurer in 2014.

cities Local governments in urban areas, run by city councils and mayors or city managers; principal responsibilities include police and fire protection, land use planning, street maintenance and construction, sanitation, libraries, and parks.

Citizens Redistricting Commission Enacted by the voters in Proposition 11 (2008), this commission is responsible for determining the boundaries of congressional and state legislative districts and Board of Equalization districts.

city council The governing body of a city; members are elected at large or by district to four-year terms.

city manager The top administrative officer in most California cities; appointed by the city council.

civil service system A system for hiring and retaining public employees on the basis of their qualifications or merit; replaced the

political machine's patronage, or spoils, system; encompasses 98 percent of state workers.

closed primary An election of party nominees in which only registered party members may participate.

collegiality Deferential behavior among justices as a way of building consensus on issues before the court.

Commission on Judicial Appointments A commission that reviews and makes recommendations on a governor's nominees for appellate and supreme courts; consists of the attorney general, the chief justice of the state supreme court, and the senior presiding judge of the courts of appeal.

Commission on Judicial Performance The state board empowered to investigate charges of judicial misconduct or incompetence.

conference committee A committee of senate and assembly members that meets to reconcile different versions of the same bill.

congressional delegation Members of the House of Representatives and Senate representing a particular state.

consolidation The merger of cities, school districts, or special districts; usually requires voter approval.

Constitution of 1849 California's first constitution, which was copied from constitutions of other states and featured a two-house legislature; a supreme court; and an executive branch including a governor, lieutenant governor, controller, attorney general, and superintendent of public instruction, as well as a bill of rights. Only white males were allowed to vote.

Constitution of 1879 California's second constitution, which retained the basic structures of the Constitution of 1849 but added institutions to regulate railroads and public utilities and to ensure fair tax assessments. Chinese individuals were denied the right to vote, own land, or work for the government.

constitutional amendments May be placed on the ballot by a two-thirds vote of the legislature or through the initiative process; must be approved by a simple majority of the voters.

contract lobbyist An individual or company that represents the interests of clients before the legislature and other policy-making entities.

contracting for services Smaller cities contract with counties, special districts, other cities, or private companies to provide services they cannot efficiently provide themselves.

controller An independently elected state executive who oversees taxing and spending.

council–manager system A form of government in which an elected council appoints a professional manager to administer daily operations; used by most California cities.

councils of government (COGs) Regional planning organizations with representation for cities and counties.

counties Local governments and administrative agencies of the state, run by elected boards of supervisors; principal responsibilities include welfare, jails, courts, roads, and elections.

county executive The top administrative officer in most California counties; appointed by the board of supervisors.

courts of appeal Three-justice panels that hear appeals from lower courts.

cross-filing An election system that allowed candidates to win the nomination of more than one political party; eliminated in 1959.

Davis, Gray Democratic governor of California (1999–2003); recalled in 2003.

de Leon, Kevin Senate president pro tem as of 2014.

demographic groups Interest groups based on race, ethnicity, gender, or age; usually concerned with overcoming discrimination.

direct democracy Progressive reforms giving citizens the power to make and repeal laws (initiative and referendum) and to remove elected officials from office (recall).

direct mail A campaign technique by which candidates communicate selected messages to selected voters by mail.

director of finance The state officer primarily responsible for preparation of the budget; appointed by the governor.

district attorney The chief prosecuting officer elected in each county; represents the people against the accused in criminal cases.

district elections Elections in which candidates are chosen by only one part of the city, county, or state.

economic groups Interest groups with sizable financial stakes in the political process who seek to influence legislators and other public policy makers.

Environmental Protection Agency (EPA) The federal government body charged with carrying out national environmental policy objectives.

executive order The power of the governor to make rules that have the effect of laws; may be overturned by the legislature.

Fair Political Practices Commission (FPPC) Established by the Political Reform Act of 1974, this independent regulatory commission monitors candidates' campaign finance reports and lobbyists.

federalism The distribution of power, resources, and responsibilities among the national, state, and local governments.

Feinstein, Dianne U.S. senator from California first elected in 1992, most recently reelected in 2012.

fiscalization of land use Cities and counties, when making land use decisions, opt for the alternative that produces the most revenue.

fragmentation Multiple local governments (counties, cities, school districts, and special districts) with no single entity responsible for governing the region as a whole.

general elections Statewide elections held on the first Tuesday after the first Monday of November in even-numbered years. Voter turnout is higher than in primary elections and highest during presidential elections.

general law city or county A city or county whose organization and structure of government are derived from state law.

general veto The gubernatorial power to reject an entire bill or budget; overruled only by an absolute two-thirds vote of both houses of the state legislature.

George, Ronald Chief justice of the California Supreme Court (1996–2011); appointed by Republican governor Pete Wilson.

ghost voting When legislators cast electronic votes in place of assembly members who are not at their posts; this practice is against the law.

governor California's highest ranking executive officeholder; elected every four years.

grants-in-aid Payments from the national government to states to assist in fulfilling public policy objectives.

gut-and-amend The process of removing the original provisions from a bill and inserting new, unrelated content, usually at the last minute.

Harris, Kamala Former attorney general elected to U.S. Senate in 2016.

incorporation The process by which residents of an urbanized area form a city.

independent expenditures Campaign spending by interest groups and political action committees on behalf of candidates.

initiative A Progressive device by which people may put laws and constitutional amendments on the ballot after securing the required number of voters' signatures.

insurance commissioner An elected state executive who regulates the insurance industry; created by a 1988 initiative.

interest group An organized group of individuals sharing common political objectives who actively attempt to influence policy makers.

isolated elections Local elections held separately from statewide elections, commonly with very low voter turnout.

item veto The power of the governor to delete or reduce the budget within a bill without rejecting the entire bill or budget; an absolute two-thirds vote of both houses of the state legislature is required to override.

Johnson, Hiram Leader of the Progressive reform movement in California; governor 1911–1917; U.S. senator 1917–1945.

Jones, Dave Elected insurance commissioner in 2010, reelected in 2014.

judicial activism Making policy through court decisions rather than through the legislative or electoral process.

Judicial Council Chaired by the chief justice of the state supreme court and composed of twenty-one judges and attorneys; makes the rules for court procedures, collects data on the courts' operations and workload, and gives seminars for judges.

legislative analyst An assistant to the legislature who studies the annual budget and proposed programs.

legislative committees Small groups of senators or assembly members who consider and make legislation in specialized areas such as agriculture or education.

legislative counsel Assists the legislature in preparing bills and assessing their impact on existing legislation.

legislative initiatives Propositions placed on the ballot by the legislature rather than by citizen petition.

lieutenant governor The chief executive when the governor is absent from the state or disabled; succeeds the governor in case of death or other departure from office; casts a tiebreaking vote in the senate; is independently elected.

litigation An interest group tactic of challenging a law or policy in the courts to have it overruled, modified, or delayed.

lobbying Interest group efforts to influence political decision makers, often through paid professionals (lobbyists).

local agency formation commission (LAFCO) A county agency set up to oversee the creation and expansion of cities.

Local Control Funding Formula A policy enacted by the state legislature in 2013 that sets aside extra K–12 education funds for poor students and English learners.

logrolling A give-and-take process in which legislators trade support for each other's bills.

mayor The ceremonial leader of a city; usually a position that alternates among council members, but in some large cities the mayor is directly elected and given substantial powers.

McCarthy, Kevin Bakersfield Republican elected majority leader of the U.S. House of Representatives in 2014.

Newsom, Gavin Former San Francisco mayor elected lieutenant governor in 2010 and reelected in 2014.

no party preference Designation chosen when voters register and decline to affiliate with a political party; sometimes referred to as "independent" voters.

nonpartisan elections A Progressive reform that removed party labels from ballots for local and judicial offices.

nonprofessional lobbyists Grassroots efforts by citizens and others intended to influence policy makers.

Padilla, Alex Former state senator elected secretary of state in 2014.

Pelosi, Nancy House minority leader; highest ranking woman in the Congress.

personal income tax A graduated tax on individual earnings adopted in 1935; the largest source of state revenues.

plea bargaining An agreement between the prosecution and the accused in which the latter pleads guilty to a reduced charge and lesser penalty.

political action committees (PACs) Mechanisms by which interest groups direct campaign contributions to preferred campaigns.

political consultants Expert professionals in political campaigning available for hire; most consultants work exclusively for candidates of one of the major political parties.

Political Reform Act of 1974 An initiative requiring officials to disclose conflicts of interest, campaign contributions, and spending; also requires lobbyists to register with the Fair Political Practices Commission.

president pro tem The legislative leader of the state senate; chairs the Rules Committee; selected by the majority party.

primary elections Elections to choose nominees for public office; held in June of even-numbered years. Voter turnout is typically low.

Progressives Members of an antimachine reform movement that reshaped the state's political institutions between 1907 and the 1920s.

property tax A tax on land and buildings; until the passage of Proposition 13 in 1978, the primary source of revenues for local governments.

Proposition 1A (2008) A $10 billion bond passed by the voters to begin construction of a high-speed rail system; officially called the Safe, Reliable High-Speed Passenger Train Bond Act for the 21st Century.

Proposition 8 (2008) An initiative that amended the state constitution to restrict marriage to opposite-sex couples.

Proposition 11, Voters FIRST Initiative (2008) An initiative that placed legislative redistricting in the hands of a fourteen-member citizens commission instead of the state legislature.

Proposition 13 (1978) Also known as the Jarvis–Gann initiative; a ballot measure that cut property taxes and significantly reduced revenues for local governments.

Proposition 22, Local Taxpayers, Public Safety, and Transportation Act (2010) An initiative that keeps the state government from taking local government funds.

Proposition 25 (2010) An initiative that lowered the votes required for the legislature to pass a budget from two-thirds to a simple majority.

Proposition 28 (2012) An initiative that allows state legislators to serve for no more than twelve years in either house of the legislature, with no restrictions on how they divide their time.

Proposition 30 (2012) Governor Brown's initiative to increase sales taxes for five years and income taxes for affluent Californians for seven years. Voters extended the increase in income tax on the affluent for twelve years in 2016.

Proposition 34 (2000) A legislative initiative setting contribution limits for individuals and political action committees.

Proposition 36 (2012) An initiative that made it easier for nonviolent "three strikes" convicts to petition for reduced sentences.

Proposition 55 (2016) An initiative passed in 2016 that continued a temporary high-end state personal income tax category through 2030, bringing in between $6 and $8 billion annually mostly for K–12 public education.

Proposition 56 (2016) An initiative that increased the cigarette tax by $2.00 per pack, with equivalent increases in other tobacco products and electronic cigarettes.

Proposition 58 (2016) An initiative to remove the ban on bilingual education passed by the voters in 1994 as part of Proposition 227.

Proposition 60 (2016) An initiative requiring performers in adult films to use condoms during explicit sex scenes. The initiative did not pass.

Proposition 61 (2016) An initiative that would have required state agencies to pay the lowest price secured by the U.S. Department of Veterans Affairs for prescription drugs. The initiative failed to pass.

Proposition 98 (1988) An initiative awarding public education a fixed percentage of the state budget.

Proposition 140 (1990) An initiative limiting assembly members to three 2-year terms and senators and statewide elected officials to two 4-year terms and cutting the legislature's budget.

Proposition 227 (1998) An initiative limiting bilingual education to no more than one year; repealed in 2016.

public defender A county officer representing defendants who cannot afford an attorney; appointed by the county board of supervisors.

public interest groups Organizations that purport to represent the general good rather than private interests.

ranked-choice voting Voters rank candidates in order of preference. If no candidate wins a majority, the candidate with the fewest votes is eliminated and those votes are assigned to the voters' second choice, and so on, until one candidate attains a majority.

Reagan, Ronald Republican governor of California (1966–1975) and U.S. president (1981–1989).

realignment The transfer of some state-provided services to counties, most recently observed with the movement of state prisoners to county jails.

recall A Progressive reform allowing voters to remove elected officials by petition and majority vote.

redistricting The adjustment of legislative district boundaries to keep all districts equal in population; done every ten years; done by a citizen commission beginning in 2011.

referendum A Progressive reform requiring the legislature to place certain measures before the voters, who may also repeal legislation by petitioning for a referendum.

register to vote Citizens who are over eighteen years of age and who are not incarcerated or in a mental institution are eligible to sign up to vote by completion of a registration form. Over 20 percent of those eligible to register in California do not do so and thus cannot participate in elections. As of 2017, voter registration will be automatic when driver's licenses are awarded or renewed.

Rendon, Anthony Speaker of the Assembly, 2015–.

Reynolds v. Sims A 1964 U.S. Supreme Court decision that ordered redistricting of the upper houses of all state legislatures by population instead of land area.

Rules Committee A five-member senate committee consisting of the senate president pro tem and two other members from each party in the senate; assigns chairs and committee appointments; functions as the gatekeeper for most senate legislation.

runoff election When no candidate receives more than 50 percent of the vote in a nonpartisan primary for trial court judge or local office, the top two candidates face each other in a runoff.

sales tax A statewide tax on most goods and products; adopted in 1933; local governments receive a portion of this tax.

school districts Local governments created by states to provide elementary and secondary education; governed by elected school boards.

Schwarzenegger, Arnold Republican governor (2003–2009) elected when Gray Davis was recalled.

secretary of state An elected state executive who keeps election records and supervises elections.

Silicon Valley The top area for high-tech industries; located between San Jose and San Francisco.

single-issue groups Organized groups with narrow policy objectives; not oriented toward compromise.

Southern Pacific Railroad A railroad company founded in 1861; developed a political machine that dominated California state politics through the turn of the century.

speaker of the assembly The legislative leader of the assembly; selected by the majority party; controls committee appointments and the legislative process.

special districts Local government agencies providing a single service, such as fire protection or sewage disposal.

special session A legislative session called by the governor; limited to discussion of topics specified by the governor.

split-ticket voting voters who do not vote a straight, party-line ticket but vote for a mix of candidates from different parties.

state auditor An assistant to the legislature who analyzes ongoing programs.

Steinberg, Darrell Senate president pro tem between 2008 and 2014.

strong-mayor form of government A form of city government in which the mayor is directly elected with powers including the veto, budget control, and appointment of department heads.

superintendent of public instruction The elected state executive in charge of public education.

superior courts Lower courts in which criminal and civil cases are first tried.

supreme court California's highest judicial body; hears appeals from lower courts.

term limits Limits on the number of terms that officeholders may serve; elected executive branch officers are limited to two 4-year terms; state legislators can serve up to a total of twelve years, in the assembly (2-year terms) or senate (4-year terms) or some combination; some local elected officials are limited to two or three 4-year terms.

termed out An elected official must leave office when he or she has completed all the terms of office allowed under California's term limits laws.

third parties Minor political parties that capture a small percentages of the vote in some elections and are viewed as important protest vehicles.

"three strikes" A 1994 law and initiative requiring sentences of twenty-five years to life for anyone convicted of three felonies.

top-two primary Voters in primary elections may cast their ballots for any listed candidate for an office irrespective of the voters' party affiliation; the top two vote winners proceed to a runoff in the general election; instituted by a 2010 ballot measure; first in effect in 2012.

Torlakson, Tom Elected superintendent of public instruction in 2010, reelected in 2014.

treasurer The elected state executive responsible for managing state funds between collection and spending.

Trust Act State legislation that prevents local law enforcement authorities from keeping illegal immigrants in custody any more than necessary.

unincorporated area An area of a county that is not part of any city.

user taxes Taxes on select commodities or services "used" by those who benefit directly from them; examples include gasoline taxes and cigarette taxes.

veto See *general veto* and *item veto*.

vote by mail Voters who prefer not to vote at their polling places or who are unable to vote on Election Day may apply to their county registrar of voters for an absentee ballot and vote by mail or register as permanent absentee voters; over half of those who vote in California elections vote by mail.

voter turnout The proportion of eligible and/or registered voters who actually participate in an election. When turnout is high, the electorate is usually more diverse and liberal; when it is low, the electorate is usually older, more affluent, and more conservative.

Warren, Earl Governor of California (1943–1953), then chief justice of the U.S. Supreme Court (1954–1969); a Republican who transcended partisan politics, taking advantage of cross-filing.

Wilson, Pete Republican governor of California (1991–1999).

Workingmen's Party Denis Kearney's antirailroad, anti-Chinese organization; instrumental in rewriting California's constitution in 1879.

Yee, Betty Elected state controller in 2014.

Index